RUNE SCAPE

THE OFFICIAL HANDBOOK

SCHOLASTIC INC.

New York   Toronto   London   Auckland   Sydney
Mexico City   New Delhi   Hong Kong   Buenos Aires

ISBN 0-439-87772-5

12 11 10 9 8 7 6 5 4 3 2 1   6 7 8 9 10/0

Designed by Christopher Morgan Long
Printed in the U.S.A.
First printing, September 2006

Table of Contents

Welcome to the World of RuneScape

This guide covers all aspects of the free to play version of RuneScape. When you enter the world of RuneScape, you enter a richly detailed world of fantasy. After you sign up, you become one of the millions of characters in RuneScape. After a short tutorial, you enter the world and interact with nonplayer characters (NPCs) and players from all over the world who have logged on to experience one of RuneScape's many adventures.

As you travel around RuneScape, you will meet Wizards, Goblins, Dwarves, and other characters and creatures. You will have the chance to learn skills such as combat, mining, cooking, and runecrafting. You will be able to make goods to sell in stores or trade with other players. You can craft ancient runes and use them in magic spells. You can become a warrior and battle for glory and riches. Just about anything you can imagine, you can do as your RuneScape character.

The Origins of RuneScape

RuneScape began in 1998 as an idea by two brothers: Paul and Andrew Gower. In 2001, the game began to be run by a company called Jagex Limited. The game changed over the years and in 2004 RuneScape became the game most players know today.

There are millions of registered players on RuneScape, and hundreds of thousands of them are playing the game at any one time. These players are from all over the world, although the game is most popular in the United States, the United Kingdom, Canada, the Netherlands, and Australia.

New skills, quests, characters, and places to visit are being added to RuneScape all the time, so a player is guaranteed a unique experience each time they play.

About This Strategy Guide

If you are just starting RuneScape, the huge world can be overwhelming. This book will help you make sense of all the different aspects of RuneScape, including:

Skills: We'll tell you what the basic skills in RuneScape are and how to master them.

Combat: RuneScape players love to battle. We'll tell you what to do if you're attacked – and how to master the skills of a warrior.

Quests: We won't tell you how to complete your quest – that would spoil the fun! But we will give you some tips and hints to help you on your way.

Characters and Creatures: Get the scoop about the many people and monsters you'll encounter in RuneScape.

Maps: Getting around RuneScape can be tricky. These maps and facts will give you an edge.

Glossary: Until you get used to the RuneScape lingo, check this quick guide to find out what everybody's talking about.

Be sure to enjoy your adventure!

Online Safety and Security Guidelines

First things first. RuneScape is an online game, which means it's a lot different from playing a game at home with your friends and family. Even though you might make friends in the game, remember that you DO NOT know these people in real life. It's important and best to keep a safe distance from other RuneScape players.

1. NEVER ever give other players your personal information. Don't tell them your real name, e-mail address, home address, or any phone numbers. If you get a message from someone claiming to work for RuneScape, don't believe it! Jagex, the company that makes RuneScape, will never ask you for this information.

2. NEVER ever make plans to meet a RuneScape player in real life. There is no way for you to know if the player is really who they say they are. If a player asks to meet with you in real life, let your parent or guardian know about it right away.

3. Using your game friends list is the safest way to chat with players. But if someone makes you feel uncomfortable, STOP chatting right away! You can block all messages from that player by clicking on the ignore button – it's a picture that looks like an unhappy face. You can also report a player in the game by clicking the report abuse button.

4. ALWAYS let a parent or guardian know what you are doing online. Spend some time showing your parents the world of RuneScape. Ask them to check on you regularly to see if you're having any problems. And if you do have a problem, share it with them.

5. Do not give your password to any other player! Period. Don't tell them your password recovery questions, either. Remember, Jagex staff will never e-mail you and ask you for your password or any other personal information. If you get an e-mail from someone claiming to be from Jagex who wants personal info, they're lying!

6. Think before using your password. Never enter your password or recovery questions into ANY Web site other than runescape.com or runescape.co.uk. When you choose your password, make sure it's different from passwords you use on other sites.

7. Watch out for fake Web sites! There are Web sites out there that claim to be official RuneScape sites, but they've actually been set up to steal your password! Don't trust a site just because it looks official. There are no secret RuneScape sites! The only sites you should log into are runescape.com or runescape.co.uk.

8. Do not use unofficial RuneScape add-ons. These are programs that claim to make RuneScape easier or better, but they actually steal your password! Besides, using programs like these are against the rules! (See Rule 7 on page 8.)

9. Watch out for fake e-mails and fake staff! There are many people out there who pretend to work for Jagex, the company that makes RuneScape. Do not trust them. If Jagex needs to send a message to RuneScape players, they will use the RuneScape Message Center.

10. Do not share your account with anyone else! Not even your best friend. First of all, it's against the rules (see Rule 6 on page 8). It's also an easy way to lose your account.

Jagex Promises:

• They never send e-mails saying they need your password to check that you aren't cheating.

• They never send e-mails saying they need your recovery questions to check you didn't steal the account.

• They never send e-mails containing attachments of any sort.

• They never send e-mails saying they need your password to let you join the Jagex staff.

• They never send e-mails offering to let you test new features or servers.

The Rules of RuneScape

Rule 1: No Offensive Language

You must not use any language that others might consider to be offensive, racist, or obscene. This includes swearing.

Rule 2: No Item Scamming

You must not trick other players into giving you their items or steal items from other players. Lying to other players for your own personal gain is not in the spirit of the game.

Rule 3: No Password Scamming

Asking or trying to persuade another player to give you their password for ANY reason is against the rules.

Rule 4: No Cheating/Bug Abuse

You must not use or attempt to use any cheats or errors that you find in Jagex's software. If you find one, report it immediately to Jagex Customer Support through the main menu.

Rule 5: No Impersonating Jagex Staff

You should not attempt to impersonate Jagex staff in any way, for any reason. Jagex staff members will have a gold crown next to their names when speaking in the game. Anyone who does not have a gold crown next to their name is not Jagex staff. This applies to both private chat and general in-game chat.

Rule 6: No Account Sharing/Trading

Each account should be used by only one person. Account sharing is not allowed. You may not sell, transfer, or lend your account to anyone else, or permit anyone else to use your account, and you may not accept an account that anybody else offers you.

Rule 7: No Macroing

You must not attempt to use other programs, such as bots, macros, or autominers to give yourself an unfair advantage in the game. You also may not circumvent any Jagex mechanisms designed to log out inactive users automatically.

Rule 8: No Multiple Log-In

You may create more than one RuneScape account, but if you do, you may not log in to more than one account at any time, and the characters must not interact with each other in any way. This includes "drop trading" or any other method of item transfer.

Rule 9: No Encouraging Others to Break Rules

You must not encourage other players to break any of the RuneScape rules.

Rule 10: No Misuse of Customer Support

You must not misuse RuneScape Customer Support. This includes threatening or reporting an innocent person, supplying false information, and abusing Jagex staff.

Rule 11: No Advertising

You are not allowed to actively advertise in the RuneScape game or RuneScape forums. This includes advertising any Web site or product, and giving out any Web address to other players is not allowed.

Rule 12: No Real-World Item Trading

RuneScape items must be exchanged only for other items/services within the game. Exchanging RuneScape items for items or other benefits in other online games, real-life money, or other real-life benefits is not allowed.

Rule 13: No Asking for Personal Details

For our players' privacy and safety, you must not ask for personal contact details such as full name, home address, or telephone number from another player. You may give very general information about yourself if you wish, such as your first name, country, and age, but please bear in mind that keeping your details to yourself keeps you and your account safe.

Rule 14: No Misuse of Official Forums

You must follow the forum codes of conduct, which are linked at the top of the forums.

Now that you know the rules, get ready to have some RuneScape fun!

Ten Tips for Beginners

1. Know Your Dots.

The little map in the corner of your screen will give you a bird's-eye view of what's happening in your location. A white dot is a player. A yellow dot is a RuneScape character. And a red dot is an object on the ground that you can pick up.

2. Explore Lumbridge.

Do a few things in this village to get used to moving around RuneScape.

3. Use Your Map.

As a new player, you will be unfamiliar with your surroundings.
That's what maps are for! Use the one you are given during the tutorial until you can easily find your way around. You'll be surprised at how helpful a good map can be!

4. Sell Your Stuff.

Just like the real world, money makes the RuneScape world go 'round. You can sell just about anything you catch or make to stores or other players. A good way to practice is to kill a chicken in Lumbridge. Chop down a tree, then cook the chicken over a fire. You can eat the cooked chicken, of course, or you can sell it to the general store for 1 GP (or gold piece). It's not much, but you can kill and cook more chickens until the GPs add up, and you'll also get experience (known as XP, or experience points, in RuneScape talk)!

5. Goblins Are Easy Targets.

There are lots of level 2 Goblins running around Lumbridge. If you slay them, they will drop money and other items – which you can pick up!

6. Know Your Specialty Shops.

The general store will buy just about anything, but if you try to sell a cooked chicken to Bob's Brilliant Axes, you'll be out of luck. If you get an item a specialty shop will buy, you might be able to get a better price for it there than at the general store.

7. Check Prices.

You can sell or trade your items to other players in the game, but be sure you don't get ripped off! A good way to check is to see what the item is selling for in stores, then sell your item for close or a little less. If you are trading, check the prices of both items to make sure they're about the same. You may also find that for certain items, higher-level players will pay even more than shop prices. It's definitely worth looking out for opportunities like this.

8. More XP Equals More GPs.

The more skilled you are at a craft, the more money you can make by selling the things you create by cooking, crafting, mining, or other skills.

9. Beware of the Wilderness.

North of Varrock is the Wilderness, where players can attack one another. If you're new, some players might lure you into the Wilderness so they can attack you. Don't go unless you're prepared. And it's good advice to leave any equipment that you don't want to lose in the bank.

10. Get to a Bank.

If by some chance your character dies (and it probably will), don't freak out. You will end up back in Lumbridge – but any GPs you were carrying will be gone. Keep most of your GPs in a bank and you will have something to fall back on in times of trouble. You can find a bank on the top floor of Lumbridge Castle.

Using Your Controls

The RuneScape tutorial will teach you the basic skills you need to know to get around the game. But there are a few additional features you will use again and again. Here are some tips to get you familiar with these controls.

Camera Controls

You can rotate the camera on your screen to get the best view of the action. Sometimes it's necessary to see objects that you'd otherwise miss. Rotating the camera is easy:

1. Press the LEFT and RIGHT arrows to rotate the camera from left to right.

2. Use the UP and DOWN arrow keys to adjust the vertical height of the camera. With this feature, you can move from a behind-the-player view to a bird's-eye view from above.

Trading with Other Players

Why should you trade items with other players? You can usually sell or buy your items at a better price than the shops offer. You can also get items through trading that might not be available in the shops. Follow these easy steps to learn how to trade:

1. Find a buyer or a seller. If you have mined some coal and want to sell it, go to a busy area and yell, "Coal for sale!"

2. If somebody wants to buy your coal, right-click on their character. Select the "Trade" option. The other player will be informed of your request. They will click on your character and also select the "Trade" option.

3. A screen will appear. The items on the left are what you are offering to trade. The items on the right are what the other player is offering. To add an item to your offer, click on it in the inventory box. To add multiples of the same object, right-click on the object. Click the "Offer x" option to select the number you wish to offer. If you want to remove an item from the trade, just click on it in the Offer window and it will be removed.

4. Are you happy with the trade? Then press the green ACCEPT button. If you change your mind, just hit DECLINE.

5. If you do accept, a final confirmation screen will appear. This gives you one last chance to check the trade you are about to complete. Make sure you are happy with what is being offered. Then press ACCEPT for the last time.

Be careful when trading! There is no way to reverse a trade once it's completed. Some players may try to trick you by saying they'll give you information in return for items, or by promising to give the item right back to you. It's best not to trust offers like this.

Shops

You can buy and sell almost anything in RuneScape's many shops. Follow these steps to make shop transactions:

1. Talk to the shopkeeper of a store and choose the "Talk-to" option. Or right-click the mouse and choose the "Trade" option. That will take you straight to the Shop screen.

2. The Shop screen will show you all of the items you can buy in the current shop. Next to each item is a number that shows how many of the item is for sale. If there is no number next to the item, that means there is only one left, so buy it quickly if you want it!

3. Check out your inventory, which will be displayed on the screen. Do you have enough room to buy what you want?

4. If you want to buy an item, left-click on it to find out how many GPs the shopkeeper wants. If you like the price, right-click and choose one of the "Buy" options. Sold!

5. If you want to sell an item to the shop, click on the item in your inventory. You will see how much the shop is willing to pay, or even if the shop wants to buy it at all. If you like the price offered, right-click on your item. Choose the number you want to sell with the "Sell" option.

Understanding Prices: If the shop has 500 swords in stock, for example, it will probably sell them to you at a low price. But if you try to sell a sword to the shop, you might not get the high price for it that you want. Wait until the shop is low on swords and try again.

Banks

Using a bank is important if you want to do a lot in RuneScape. You can carry only 28 items in your inventory at a time (not including weapons and clothing). If you die, you will lose whatever GPs you are carrying. So using a bank allows you to store extra inventory and keep your GPs safe.

Here's how to use the RuneScape banks:

1. Find and walk to the nearest bank. When you get there, right-click on any of the booths there. The bank screen will appear. Now you can choose to deposit and withdraw items.

2. Any items you have deposited in the bank will appear on the screen. If you have more than one of an item, the number will appear next to it.

3. To deposit an item, right-click on the item in your inventory and choose the "Deposit" option. Select the number you wish to deposit from the list. It's that easy!

4. If you want to withdraw an item from your inventory, you will have two choices. You can simply withdraw the item. If it is a tradeable item that does not stack in your inventory, such as ore or food, you can withdraw it as a "Note." The advantage of this is that the item won't take up a lot of space in your inventory, but you can still sell or trade it. For the most part, though, you can't use or wield an item that has been withdrawn as a note.

5. The SWAP and INSERT buttons on the screen are there to help you organize your screen. If you choose SWAP, just drag and drop an item on your Bank screen on top of another item; they will swap positions. Choose INSERT to drag and drop an item to a new place; the items will shuffle positions to make room for it.

Friends

You can keep in contact with the other players you make friends with in RuneScape by using your Friends List. It's easy:

1. Click on the smiley face on your player interface to call up the Friends List screen.

2. To add a friend to the list, click on the button marked ADD FRIENDS and type in the name of the player you want to add. You can also right-click on the name of a player in a Chat window and select the appropriate option.

3. To remove a friend from the list, just click on the DEL FRIEND button and type in the name of the player you want to remove.

Ignoring Players

You can also prevent other players from messaging you if you don't want to hear from them. That's easy, too:

1. Click on the sad-face button on your player interface to call up the Ignore List screen.

2. To add a player to the list, click on the button marked ADD NAME and type in the name of the player you want to add. You can also right-click on the name of a player in a Chat window and select the correct option.

Chat Options

There are three options on the bottom of the RuneScape screen that control how other players interact with you:

1. "Public Chat": This controls how much chat you can receive from other players. Choose from ON, FRIEND ONLY, OFF, or HIDE.

2. "Private Chat": This controls how players contact you with private messages. If set to ON, anyone can contact you, whether they are a friend or not. You can also choose FRIENDS ONLY and OFF.

3. "Trade/Complete": This controls whether other players can send you trade requests or challenge you to duels. The options are ON, FRIENDS ONLY, or OFF.

Taking Your Own Screenshots

Want to remember a moment from your game forever? Here's how you can take screenshots from your game, so you can show your friends your most awesome RuneScape accomplishments. Taking screenshots is super easy, but how you do it depends on whether you use Windows or a Macintosh operating system.

If you use Windows:

1. Press the PRINT SCREEN key on your keyboard. This is located next to the F12 key. Pressing this will put whatever is on your screen onto your computer's clipboard.

2. Then open up a graphics program such as Paint or Photoshop. Paste your screenshot by pressing CTRL + V.

3. Save your picture. To make it a smaller file size, try saving it as a .gif or .png file.

If you use Macintosh:

1. Press down the SHIFT + COMMAND (apple) + 3 keys.

2. What happens next depends on which Mac system you use. If you use Mac OS 10.x, a .pdf file with your screenshot in it will be saved to your desktop. You can then open it and choose "Export" from the File menu. Then pick a new format to save it as. If you use Mac OS 9.x and below, your screenshot will be saved as an image on your desktop.

The Members Version of the Game

As you play the game, you may come across messages such as, "You need to be on a members server to use this feature." RuneScape membership requires you to pay a monthly subscription fee of $5. This will give you access to many new game features, including skills such as agility, fletching, herblore, thieving, slayer, and farming. It also expands many of the free server skills and also gives access to many new quests, items, towns, dungeons, minigames, and more.

This handbook covers the free version of the game, which you can play for as long as you like with no obligation to become a member. But if you do feel you're ready for a new challenge, becoming a member might be for you.

Mastering Basic Skills

Ever dream of being a warrior fighting for justice? A wizard casting spells? A fisherman rubbing elbows with pirates? In RuneScape you can do all of these things and more – if you master the skills needed to do it.

There are 11 basic skills in the RuneScape world:

Woodcutting
Firemaking
Fishing
Cooking
Ranging
Mining
Smithing
Crafting
Runecrafting
Magic
Prayer

We'll explore each of these skills in this section. But all of the skills work the same way. The more you practice, the more experience points, or XP, you will earn. As you earn XP, you will get better at your skill. You will be able to do the skill more quickly and easily. You will also have items and abilities open to you as you increase.

Mastering a skill is not that easy. It takes lots of time and patience. For that reason, you may want to focus on one or two skills to master. The information in this section should help you decide what skill is right for you.

As you are mastering your skills, you will meet other players mastering the skill, too. If you're doing something really time consuming, like mining or fishing, players will chat with one another. This is a good way to get pointers from other players. As your XP increases, you can share what you've learned with newer players.

When you are practicing a skill, another player might ask, "lvls"? They want to know what level you've reached with this skill.

Mastering the Basic Skill of Woodcutting

Icon	Tree	Level
	Ordinary	1
	Oak	5
	Willow	30
	Yew	60

Why Should I Master Woodcutting?

Woodcutting is just what it sounds like – cutting down trees to make logs. It's a basic skill, but it's essential. You need logs to make fire, and you need fire to cook food. You could go through the entire game just cutting down ordinary trees, but it doesn't hurt to build your woodcutting XP. Let's say you're stuck in the middle of a bunch of willow trees and you don't have enough XP to chop them down. You'd have to go searching for a lower-level tree to chop. There's another bonus, too. The higher your woodcutting XP, the more logs you'll be able to chop. Then you can sell the extras and make a profit!

What Kind of Trees Can I Chop Down?

The chart above shows what level is needed to cut down certain trees.

How Do I Do It?

It's pretty simple: Just left-click on a tree and select "Chop." Of course, you need an axe in your inventory to do the cutting. The more powerful your axe, the better chance you'll have of chopping down the tree.

How Can I Get Axes?

You will get a free axe when you do the tutorial in the game. Axes can break fairly easily, though, so you'll probably need a new one before long. If you don't have an axe, the woodsman tutor northeast of Lumbridge Castle will give you a new one, or try Bob's Brilliant Axes in Lumbridge. You'll definitely need to upgrade your axe once your skills improve; powerful axes will allow you to chop down trees much faster.

Mastering the Basic Skill of Firemaking

Why Should I Master Firemaking?

When you don't have a high firemaking XP, you can fail to light a fire quickly. A higher XP will also allow you to light a wider variety of logs. Sure, you could always cook your food on a range, but a range won't always be nearby. With strong firemaking skills, you can light a fire outdoors pretty much whenever you want. That can come in handy if your Hitpoints, or HPs, are running low, and you want to cook some meat in a hurry to regain your strength.

How Do I Do It?

You need two things to light a fire: logs and a tinderbox. Drop some logs on the ground, then click on the tinderbox in your inventory. Use the tinderbox and wait for the sparks to fly!

What Kind of Wood Can I Use?

The chart to the right shows what level is required to light different types of wood.

Icon	Wood type	Level
	Normal	1
	Oak	15
	Willow	30
	Yew	60

Mastering the Basic Skill of Fishing

Why Should I Master Fishing?

When you need to heal yourself, you need food. Fishing is a quick way of getting the food you need. Players who battle a lot especially value expensive fish like lobster and swordfish, which heal more HPs than fish like shrimp and sardines. If you master fishing, you can sell fish to these players and watch your GPs multiply!

How Do I Do It?

You'll need to find a fishing spot. Once you get there, right-click to see what options there are, or left-click to perform the default option. Net, Bait, Harpoon, Lure, and Cage. If you have the necessary equipment in your inventory, click on the option and try to catch the fish. The kind of fish you can catch depends on your fishing level. If you don't have the right equipment, you can buy it from a fishing shop. Try Gerrant's Fishing Business in Port Sarim.

What Types of Fishing Can I Master?

Type	Location	Required Items	Extra Cost
Net Fishing	Many sea fishing locations	Net	None
Sea Bait Fishing	Many sea fishing locations	Fishing rod, Fishing bait	None
Fly Fishing	Many river fishing locations	Fly Fishing rod, Feathers	1 feather every time you catch a fish
River Bait Fishing	Many river fishing locations	Fishing rod, Fishing bait	1 bait every time you catch a fish
Harpoon Fishing	Karamja Island	Harpoon	None
Lobster Fishing	Karamja Island	Cage, Lobster	None

What Kinds of Fish Can I Catch?

This chart shows you the types of fish you can catch in the game, and the level needed to catch each type.

Icon	Fish	How To Catch	Level
	Shrimp	Net Fishing	1
	Sardine	Sea Bait Fishing	5
	Herring	Sea Bait Fishing	10
	Anchovies	Net Fishing	15
	Trout	Fly Fishing	20
	Pike	River Bait Fishing	25
	Salmon	Fly Fishing	30
	Tuna	Harpoon Fishing	35
	Lobster	Lobster Fishing	40
	Swordfish	Harpoon Fishing	50

Mastering the Basic Skills of Cooking

Why Should I Master Cooking?

When you cook, you can eat food, and when you eat food, it will heal lost HPs (Hitpoints). Knowing how to cook your own food is essential early in the game. It's also very handy later on if you need to eat something and can't afford to buy something to eat. As you gain more cooking XP, you'll become a better cook. You won't burn your food as much, and you'll be able to make more complicated and interesting dishes as you progress.

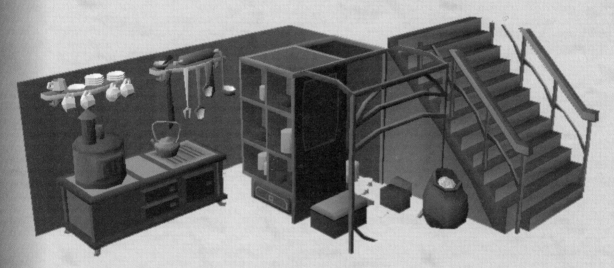

You'll also be able to cook a greater variety of foods. Let's say you've got high fishing XP and can catch lobsters. You can't cook them without a cooking level of 40! If you want to sell your lobster rather than eat it, you'll probably get more money for a cooked one. You'll also be able to cook energy-packed foods like anchovy pizza, which is great for healing yourself after a battle. You can also sell your high-level creations to rake in the GPs.

Where Can I Cook Food?

Almost every city and village in RuneScape has a range you can use to cook your food. You can also cook over an open fire if you've got some logs and a tinderbox.

Can I Join a Guild?

Sure, if you have level 32 cooking! The cooking guild is located west of Varrock. Once you enter, you'll have access to a flour mill, water, ranges, ingredients, and supplies like dishes and pans. Besides the level requirement, you need to wear a chef's hat before you can enter.

What Items Can I Cook?

This chart shows you the different foods you can cook, the level needed, and the amount of healing delivered to your Hitpoints (HPs) once you cook the food.

Icon	Food	Cooking Level	Heals
	Anchovies	1	1
	Meat	1	1
	Shrimp	1	3
	Chicken	1	3
	Sardine	1	4
	Bread	1	5
	Herring	5	5
	Redberry Pie	10	9
	Trout	15	7
	Pike	20	8
	Meat Pie	20	11
	Salmon	25	9

RuneScape Recipes

You can whip up these tasty dishes with a few ingredients and some heat!

Bread

1. Pick some grain. Take it to a windmill to make flour.

2. Use a pot to pick up the flour you have made.

3. Buy a bucket or a jug and fill it with water from a sink or fountain.

4. Mix the flour and water to make bread dough.

5. Bake the dough in a range.

Pie

1. Mix flour (see Bread above) and water to make pastry dough.

2. Place the dough in an empty pie dish.

3. Add your choice of filling to the empty pie: redberry, apple, or meat.

4. Bake the pie in a range.

Cake

1. Mix flour (see Bread on page 22), eggs, and milk together in a cake tin.

2. Bake the cake in a range.

3. Buy some chocolate and add it to the cake. (optional)

Stew

1. Get a bowl and fill it with water from a sink or fountain.

2. Pick a potato and place it in the bowl.

3. Cook some meat and add it to the bowl.

4. Cook the stew in a range or over a fire.

Pizza

1. Mix flour (see Bread on page 22) and water to make a pizza base.

2. Buy a tomato and add it to the pizza.

3. Buy some cheese and add it to the pizza.

4. Cook the pizza in a range.

5. Add your choice of topping to the pizza.

Icon	Food	Cooking Level	Heals
	Stew	25	11
	Tuna	30	10
	Apple Pie	30	14
	Wine	35	11
	Pizza	35	14
	Lobster	40	12
	Cake	40	12
	Swordfish	45	14
	Meat Pizza	45	16
	Chocolate Cake	50	15
	Anchovy Pizza	55	18

Mastering the Basic Skill of Ranging

Why Should I Master Ranging?

The ranging skill allows you to attack players or monsters from a distance, using special weapons, such as a bow and arrow. When you hit a foe from a distance, you can use hit-and-run tactics to avoid damage in the battle. It's also a good skill to know when you are fighting magic users, because it can be very effective against Mages. Another bonus is that with high ranging XP, you get to wear cool armor!

How Do I Do It?

First, you need the right equipment: a bow and some arrows or bolts to shoot from it. To use the weapons in battle, left-click on the item and chose the "Wield" option. Then click to attack a monster or another player and you will shoot your arrows or bolts until you do something else or are attacked. It's important that there be a clean line of sight between you and your target. If there is something in the way, you won't be able to attack.

After you attack, your opponent will try to run right at you for some hand-to-hand combat. If your opponent does not have any ranged attacks, you can keep shooting without taking any damage. When the fight is over, you can pick up any arrows on the ground and use them again (unless they are broken).

Icon	Bow Type	Level
	Standard	1
	Oak	5
	Willow	20
	Maple	30

A good Ranger will use the land around him to get an advantage over his opponents. Attacking from higher ground or from the other side of a fence, for example, will keep your opponent at a distance so you can keep using your ranging attacks.

What Types of Bows Can I Wield?

The chart to the left shows you the types of bows available and the level needed to wield them.

What Kinds of Ranging Armor Can I Wield?

This chart shows the types of armor Rangers can wear and the level needed to wield the armor.

Icon	Armor Type	Level
	Plain leather items	1
	Hard leather body	1 (plus 10 Defence)
	Studded leather body	20 (plus 10 Defence)
	Studded chaps	20
	Coif	20
	Green Dragonhide body	40 (plus 40 Defence)
	Green Dragonhide chaps	40
	Green Dragonhide vambrace	40

A vambrace is a piece of Rangers' armor, used to protect the forearm. When equipped, it occupies the hand slot.

Mastering the Basic Skill of Mining

Why Should I Master Mining?

The mining skill is used to get ores and metals from rocks. You can sell the ores and metals or use them to make weapons or other items. Weapons are in high demand in RuneScape, so a skilled miner will have an advantage in the game.

The higher your mining level, the more valuable metals and ores you can mine. With level 40, for example, you can mine gold to sell or to craft into valuable jewelry. Other ores, such as mithril, adamantite, and runite, are prized for making highly effective weapons. If you can master mining these metals, you'll be sought after by other players.

How Do I Do It?

First, you need a pickaxe. You will receive one during the tutorial and can get a replacement from the mining tutor, south of Lumbridge. Eventually you will want a better pickaxe. You can purchase many kinds at the pickaxe shop in the Dwarven Mines. Once you have a pickaxe, head to one of the mining sites in RuneScape to start mining rocks. Right-click on a rock and then click on the "Prospect" option. That will tell you what kinds of ores are in the rock. Then click the "Mine" option to mine the ore. The kind of ore you can mine depends on the level of mining XP you have (see the chart on page 27). It's not easy to get ore from rocks, so keep trying until you succeed. Once your mining XP increases, mining will be easier.

Icon	Type	Level
	Bronze pickaxe	1
	Iron pickaxe	1
	Steel pickaxe	6
	Mithril pickaxe	21
	Adamant pickaxe	31
	Rune pickaxe	41

Once someone has mined a rock, there will be no ore available from it for a short while. Wait a bit, and you can mine the rock again.

Can I Join a Guild?

You can enter the mining guild in Falador if your mining is level 60 or above. You will find a number of items useful for miners, including coal rocks and mithril rocks. You will also have access to the main Dwarven Mines from there.

What Kinds of Ores and Metals Can I Mine?

This chart shows the types of ores and metals found in rocks, and the level you need to mine them.

You need to complete the Rune Mysteries quest before you can mine Rune essence.

Icon	Ore	Level
	Rune essence	1
	Clay	1
	Copper ore	1
	Tin ore	1
	Iron ore	15
	Silver ore	20
	Coal	30
	Gold ore	40
	Mithril ore	55
	Adamantite Ore	70
	Runite ore	85

Mastering the Basic Skill of Smithing

Why Should I Master Smithing?

If you want to create something with the metals you've mined, you should learn how to smith. Smithing allows you to create a variety of weapons and armor, which are in high demand from other players. It's a good way to make GPs while building up your XP.

A good strategy would be to develop your mining and smithing skills at the same time. If you can combine a high mining level with a great smithing level, you'll be able to create powerful weapons that every player in RuneScape will want!

How Do I Do It?

Smithing has two stages: smelting and forging. Smelting converts your ores into bars. First, you need an ore. (If you mine your own ore, you'll save GPs and gain experience at the same time.) Go to a furnace and select an ore from your inventory. Left-click on the furnace to choose the kind of bar you want to make from your ore. You can smelt more than one kind of ore together.

Once you have made your bar, you'll need to forge it. First, you'll need a hammer, which you can buy at a general store. Head to an anvil. Select a bar from your inventory, then click on the anvil. You will be given a list of items you can make from your bar. If you don't have enough bars to make the item, it will be written in red. If the item is written in green, you're all set. Choose the item you want, then hammer away.

What Kinds of Bars Can I Make?

The chart above shows you how to combine ores to make bars. Each bar requires a different level of experience in order to smelt it.

Icon	Bar	Ores Required	Level
	Bronze	1 Tin ore, 1 Copper ore	1
	Iron	1 Iron ore	15
	Silver	1 Silver ore	20
	Steel	2 Coal, 1 Iron ore	30
	Gold	1 Gold ore	40
	Mithril	4 Coal, 1 Mithril ore	50
	Adamantite	6 Coal, 1 Adamantite ore	70
	Runite	8 Coal, 1 Runite ore	85

When you forge an iron bar, you will have only a 50 percent chance of success.

What Kinds of Items Can I Forge?

This chart shows at what level you can forge various items.

Icon	Item	Bronze	Iron	Steel	Mithril	Adamant	Rune
	Dagger	1	15	30	50	70	85
	Hatchet	1	16	31	51	71	86
	Mace	2	17	32	52	72	87
	Medium helm	3	18	33	53	73	88
	Short sword	4	19	34	54	74	89
	Nails	4	19	34	54	74	89
	Scimitar	5	20	35	55	75	90
	Long sword	6	21	36	56	76	91
	Full helm	7	22	37	57	77	92
	Square shield	8	23	38	58	78	93
	Warhammer	9	24	39	59	79	94
	Battle-axe	10	25	40	60	80	95
	Chainmail body	11	26	41	61	81	96
	Kite shield	12	27	42	62	82	97
	Two-handed sword	14	29	44	64	84	99
	Platemail legs	16	31	46	66	86	99
	Platemail skirt	16	31	46	66	86	99
	Platemail body	18	33	48	68	88	99

About Armor

A *helm* is a type of helmet. *Platemail* is a type of body armor made from plates of metal. *Chainmail* is also a type of body armor, made of small metal rings linked together.

Mastering the Basic Skill of Crafting

Why Should I Master Crafting?

You can make a lot of GPs forging metals and ores into weapons, and you can also use the skill of crafting to turn metals into jewelry. Players love to adorn their characters with necklaces and amulets, so a master jewelry maker can become a very wealthy player.

Crafting also has many practical applications. If you love cooking, you can craft your own pie dishes. If you like to battle, knowing how to craft leather armor is a handy skill.

How Do I Do It?

There are different methods for crafting different items:

Pottery: Start with clay, which you can get by mining. Soften the clay with water. Take the clay to a potter's wheel (try the Barbarian Village). Use the clay on the potter's wheel and select what object you want to make. If you have the necessary level, you will be able to make the item. Take the item to a pottery oven to fire it. If it doesn't crack upon heating, you'll end up with a nice piece of pottery.

Leather: Start with cowhides, which you can get by going to a cow field and killing some cows. Take the cowhide to Ellis the tanner in Al-Kharid. There you can turn the hide into normal or hard leather. Hard leather is stronger but costs a little more to make. Once you turn your hide into leather, you can craft it into a useful item, like a pair of boots or piece of armor. If you have enough thread in your inventory, click on the item you want to make to craft it.

Gems: If you are lucky enough to find a gem (during a Random Event, for instance), you can make it more valuable by cutting it. You can use a cut gem when you are making gold jewelry. First, buy a chisel from a general store or crafting shop. Select the chisel from your inventory and then the gem you wish to cut. If your crafting level is not high enough to cut the gem, you might want to make some more pottery to increase your XP.

Symbols: You can use silver bars to make symbols that will make your prayers last longer. These are called holy symbols. Use your silver bar on a furnace to make your holy symbol. To finish the symbol, you will need to make some string. Use shears (from

What Kinds of Items Can I Craft?

Icon	Item	Level
	Leather gloves	1
	Pot	1
	Gold ring	5
	Gold necklace	6
	Pie dish	7
	Leather boots	7
	Gold amulet	8
	Bowl	8
	Leather cowl	9
	Leather vambraces	11
	Leather body	14
	Holy symbol	16
	Leather chaps	18
	Cut sapphire	20
	Sapphire ring	22
	Sapphire necklace	22
	Tiara	23
	Sapphire amulet	24
	Cut emerald	27
	Emerald ring	27
	Hard leather body	28
	Emerald necklace	29
	Emerald amulet	31
	Cut ruby	34
	Ruby ring	34
	Ruby necklace	40
	Cut diamond	43
	Diamond ring	43
	Ruby amulet	50
	Diamond necklace	56
	Diamond amulet	70

a general store) to get wool from a sheep. Spin the wool on a spinning wheel into a ball. Use your ball of wool on your holy symbol to give it a string. If you have a prayer level of 31 or higher, you can take the symbol to Brother Jered in the Monastery to be blessed.

Jewelry and amulets: You need gold bars to make jewelry. The best way to get them is by mining and smithing. Once you have your bars, you can make amulets, necklaces, and rings. First, buy the mold you want from a crafting shop. Take the gold bar to a furnace and select the "Use" option. Then choose the item you would like to make. If you are lucky enough to have a gem, you can add this jewel to your piece if you have a high enough smithing level. If you have a high enough magic level, you can also enchant amulets that will give bonuses to their owner. First you need to give your amulet a string (see Symbols above). Then use the magic skill to enchant it (see page 34).

Can I Join a Guild?

You can enter the crafting guild if your crafting level is at least 40. You also must be wearing a brown apron. It's located west of Port Sarim and north of Rimmington. In the guild you will find many things to help you with crafting, including a pottery oven, potter's wheels, spinning wheels, gold and silver rocks, and a tanner.

You can craft a tiara as a fabulous fashion accessory – or enchant one to allow you quicker access to temples (see page 35).

Mastering the Basic Skill of Runecrafting

Why Should I Master Runecrafting?

The game is called RuneScape, after all! Once you learn to craft runes, you can use them with the magic skill to cast spells. If you want to be a master magician, then you should really know runecrafting. Sure, you can buy runes in shops, but some of the really powerful ones are rare. With a high enough runecrafting XP, you can make them yourself!

How Do I Do It?

Before you can craft runes, you must complete the Rune Mysteries quest (see page 48). Then you will have the ability to mine rune essence. You won't find rune essence in any old rock, so look for nonplayer characters (also called NPCs for short) to take you there. Once you find a rock with rune essence, mine it with a pickaxe. Then take the essence to a temple to turn it into a magical rune.

Talisman	Icon	Temple
Earth		Earth
Air		Air
Water		Water
Fire		Fire
Body		Body
Mind		Mind

Finding rune temples isn't easy, either, but you can locate them with the help of a runecrafting talisman. To locate each temple, take the talisman and select the "Locate" option. The talisman will pull in the direction of the rune temple. Runecrafting is a lost skill, so when you find the temple, it will be in ruins. Use your talisman on these ruins to be transported to a restored temple. There you will be able to turn your rune essences into rune stones.

These talismans are fairly easy to find. Look for NPCs to give them to you. But be aware – there are other, higher-level talismans available for serious seekers only!

How Can I Get to the Temples Faster?

If you've already discovered a talisman for a particular temple, you can enchant a tiara to make getting there faster. You can make a regular tiara by using a silver bar at a furnace – but first you'll need a tiara mold purchased from a crafting store. Take the tiara to the temple you want access to. For example, to make an Air tiara, take an unenchanted tiara and an Air talisman to the Air temple. Once the talisman is enchanted, you can wear it when you go to the temple ruins. Then just click on the ruins to enter. This is slightly quicker, and it also frees up room in your inventory.

What Are the Elemental Tiaras?

For faster, easier access to temples, enchant a tiara to gain access to the corresponding temple.

Earth tiara	Air tiara	Water tiara	Fire tiara	Body tiara	Mind tiara

What Kinds of Runes Can I Craft?

The chart to the left shows the types of runes you can craft and the level you need to craft them.

Icon	Rune Type	Level
	Air	1
	Mind	2
	Water	5
	Earth	9
	Fire	13
	Body	20

Mastering the Basic Skill of Magic

Why Should I Master Magic?

It's fun to be a wizard! But if you're looking for a more serious reason, consider this: Magic spells cast with runes can give you a real advantage in battle. You can attack foes from a distance and destroy them before they even know what hit them. You can also cast spells to confuse and weaken your opponents – something nonmagical foes can't do. And if your opponent is wearing heavy armor, it actually puts him at a disadvantage. Armor can make the spells you use even more effective!

How Do I Do It?

Almost all magic spells need runes. First, click on the Spell Book in your inventory to get the Magic menu. You'll see a bunch of pictures representing spells. If the picture is darkened, it means you don't have a high enough magic level to cast the spell or enough runes in your inventory. If the spell is lit up, it means you have everything you need. You're in business!

Run your cursor over the spell to get a description of it and pictures of the rune you will need. You'll also see two numbers. The number on the left shows how many of that rune you have, and the number on the right shows how many you need to cast the spell.

No two spells are alike. Some can be cast only on unfriendly monsters, and others can be cast only on yourself or your inventory. Try out a few and see what happens. If your spell fails, don't worry. That happens sometimes. You will still get XP from casting it, and you will fail less often as you gain more XP.

What Kinds of Runes Can I Use?

This chart tells you a little bit about each of the runes and what they do.

Icon	Rune	What Should I Know?
	Earth rune	One of the four elemental runes. Can be replaced by a staff of earth.
	Air rune	One of the four elemental runes. Can be replaced by a staff of air.
	Water rune	One of the four elemental runes. Can be replaced by a staff of water.
	Fire rune	One of the four elemental runes. Can be replaced by a staff of fire.
	Body rune	Required for curse spells.
	Mind rune	Required for strike spells.

While Runecrafting cosmic, nature, chaos, law, and death runes is not possible on the free game, it is possible for free players to obtain and use them. You may purchase them in shops or get them from monster drops. These can be used to cast spells for things – such as teleporting – which are unrelated to combat.

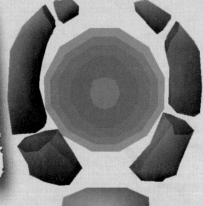

What's the Deal with Staffs?

Staffs are a quicker way to cast spells than using runes. They have an option called "Recast" which lets you cast a spell repeatedly during a battle.
First, you need to wield a staff. Select the Combat Style menu, which is represented by crossed swords. Choose any of the elemental spells you want to use and tie them to your staff. Then select the "Attack With" option on your staff and you will automatically fight by casting that spell when you enter combat.

What Kinds of Jewelry Can I Enchant?

If you have the necessary magic levels, you can enchant ordinary pieces of jewelry and make them magical items. This chart shows what happens when you enchant different types of jewelry.

Icon	Item	Level to Enchant	Effect When Equipped	Length of Enchantment
	Amulet of Magic	7	While worn, player's magic attack is boosted by 10.	Permanent. Works whenever it is equipped.
	Amulet of Defence	27	While worn, player's defence is boosted by 7.	Permanent. Works whenever it is equipped.
	Amulet of Strength	49	While worn, player's strength is boosted by 10.	Permanent. Works whenever it is equipped.
	Amulet of Power	57	While worn, player's attack, strength, and defence are boosted by 6.	Permanent. Works whenever it is equipped.

Mastering the Basic Skill of Prayer

Why Should I Master Prayer?

Magic is one way to give you an edge in RuneScape. Prayer is another. It's a special skill made up entirely for the RuneScape game. It can give you a boost in battle, make you stronger, and restore Hitpoints. It doesn't cost you a thing, but the effects don't last long.

How Do I Do It?

It's easy to use prayer – just select the prayer symbol from your interface. If you are at a high enough level to use a prayer, it will be lit up. Left-click on the prayer to activate it. Your prayer points will drain when you use prayers, so head to a church to recharge them. One way to increase your prayer XP is to bury the bones of monsters you kill! (Or you can bury bones left on the ground by another player.)

Can I Join a Guild?

No, but if you have a prayer level of 31 or more, you can enter the monastery located west of Edgeville. You can get a prayer boost here and grab some monk's robes, too.

Mastering Combat

Why Should I Battle?

Let's face it – the combat option is one of the most popular features on RuneScape. It's a way for ordinary people to unleash their inner warrior in a safe environment. In RuneScape, you can slay monsters and battle fierce warriors in competitions of skill and strength.

Whether or not you want to fight, it's a good idea to build up your overall combat level. You never know when a Skeleton, Scorpion, or some other creature will attack you out of nowhere. It's good to know how to defend yourself.

How Do I Do It?

To fight a monster or character in the game, just point your mouse at your opponent and select the "Attack" option. Not all characters can be attacked, and you can't attack other players unless you're in the Wilderness. If you're able to attack a character, you'll see their combat level next to their name.

Then it's time to make a decision. If your opponent's combat level is a lot higher than yours, you probably don't want to fight. There are color codes to help you: A weaker opponent will have a green number, an equal opponent will have a yellow number, and a strong opponent will have a red number.

If you decide to fight, click on the crossed swords icon on your player interface. This will show what weapons you have and what moves you can do with them. When you choose your move, the battle begins!

How Do I Know If I'm Winning or Losing?

Each fighting character will have a horizontal bar above his head. The color green means you're healthy. If the bar starts turning red, it means you're taking damage. If your bar is red, and your opponent's is still pretty green, you can run away from the battle if you want. Keep moving, because monsters will chase you when you run!

What Happens If I Die?

Don't panic. If you lose all of your Hitpoints in a battle, your character will "die." But you won't be out of the game. You'll soon turn up in Lumbridge, alive and well. You will keep all of your stats and skills, but you'll lose all of the items you're carrying! That's why it's a good idea to keep most of your stuff in the bank.

There is a bonus for nonviolent players: If you haven't attacked any other players recently, you will get to keep your three most valuable items when your character dies.

Ranging (page 24) and magic (page 34) skills can also be used in combat.

What Kinds of Combat Skills Do I Have?

Skill	What It Does	How to Build it Up
Attack	Advancing this skill increases your chances of hitting an opponent.	You can concentrate on training your Attack skill by selecting "Accurate" attack styles.
Strength	Advancing this skill increases the amount of damage you can do.	You can concentrate on training your Strength skill by selecting "Aggressive" attack styles.
Defence	Advancing this skill decreases your chances of being hit by an opponent.	You can concentrate on training your Defence skill by selecting "Defencive" attack styles.
Hitpoints	This is the amount of damage you can take before your character dies.	Your Hitpoints will increase as you get more combat experience.

What Are Some Battle Strategies I Can Use?

Here are some things to know when battling different types of players.

Skill	Good Against	Bad Against	Tip
Fighter	Rangers, who have trouble penetrating their plate armor.	Mages, who can attack from a distance. Plate armor conducts magic.	When fighting a Mage, a Fighter should remove plate armor, then try to run in for some close combat
Mage	Fighters. A Mage will attack from a safe distance. His spells will be made stronger by the Fighter's plate armor.	Rangers. Their leather armor is a good defense against spells. And a Mage's robes are not arrow-proof.	When facing a Fighter, a Mage should blast away with his best damage spells and hope for the best!
Ranger	Mages. Rangers' leather armor is a good defense against spells, and a longbow can snag a Mage as he's running away.	Fighter, although it's a close fight. A Fighter's plate armor can't be penetrated by arrows. If a fighter gets close enough, he will hack through a Ranger's leather armor with his powerful weapons.	A Ranger should be sure to keep his distance when fighting a Fighter. If all else fails, he can distract the Fighter and run away.

What Types of Weapons Can I Wield?

This chart shows the different types of weapons available and how they compare to one another when used in combat.

Icon	Weapon	Speed	Strength	Damage
	Dagger	Fast	Weak	Stab/Slash
	Short sword	Fast	Weak	Stab
	Scimitar	Fast	Medium	Slash/Stab
	Mace	Medium	Weak	Crush/Stab
	Long sword	Medium	Medium	Slash/Stab
	Hatchet	Medium	Weak	Slash/Crush
	Pickaxe	Medium	Weak	Stab/Crush
	Battle-axe	Slow	High	Slash/Crush
	Warhammer	Slow	High	Crush
	Two-handed sword	Slowest	Highest	Slash/Crush

Why Do I Need Armor?

If you're going to be in battle, you're going to need some armor to protect you. You can buy armor in a shop, or learn how to make it with the skills of smithing and crafting. The kind of armor you wear depends on the kind of fighting you want to do.

Fighting Armor

Armor for melee Fighters is made from a wide range of materials, usually metals. These are the types of armor available for Fighters:

Icon	Armor	Advantage	Disadvantage
	Full helmet	Offers good protection from attacks.	Can obstruct your vision.
	Medium helmet	Easier to see what you're doing	Offers less protection than a full helmet
	Chainmail	Flexible. Good against slashing weapons and crushing attacks.	Not effective against stabbing weapons and small pointy blades.
	Plate armor	Stronger than chainmail. Good against slashing and stabbing attacks.	Weak against crushing attacks. Makes it difficult to fire arrows or cast spells.
	Kite Shield	Good against slashing attacks.	Weak against crushing attacks.

Icon	Metal	Attack Level
	Bronze	1
	Iron	1
	Steel	5
	Black	10
	Mithril	20
	Adamant	30
	Rune	40

Metal Attack-Level Requirements

Your weapons can be made from different metals, depending on what your attack level is.

Icon	Metal	Defence Level
	Bronze	I
	Iron	I
	Steel	5
	Black	10
	Mithril	20
	Adamant	30
	Rune	40

Metal Defence Level Requirements

Similarly, armor can be made from different metals, depending on what your defence level is.

Ranger Armor

This chart shows what kinds of armor are available to Rangers, and what level you need to wear it.

Icon	Armor Type	Ranged Level
	Plain leather items	I
	Hard leather body	I (plus 10 Defence)
	Studded leather body	20 (plus 20 Defence)
	Studded chaps	20
	Coif	20
	Green Dragonhide	40 (plus 40 Defence)

Leather and Dragonhide?

Leather

Advantage: Can be toughened with hardening or studs. Flexible. Resistant to crushing attacks.

Disadvantage: Weaker against stabbing attacks.

Dragonhide

Advantage: Much stronger than basic leather. Can help defend against spells and magical effects.

Disadvantage: Can interfere with the wearer's ability to cast magic.

Mage Armor

Because heavy armor will interfere with the casting of magic spells, it doesn't really work very well for Mages. Mage Robes are a better option. They allow you to easily cast and defend against magic. One limitation, however, is that they offer no protection against ranged or melee combat.

Mastering Quests

Why Should I Go on Quests?

No matter what you choose to do in RuneScape – whether you're a Fighter, a fisherman, or a Mage – there is something you can gain by going on quests. It's a great way to get to know RuneScape and practice your skills, and if you succeed, there's always a reward waiting for you.

As you travel around RuneScape, you may see this 🔵 quest icon. If you do, talk to the NPCs in the area of the icon. A nearby character will usually start you on your quest.

Of course, some quests are challenging, and there are dangers lurking in some quests that could seriously harm your hitpoints. That's why we've provided you with this guide to the quests of RuneScape. We'll tell you where to find them and what's at stake, and give you some hints and tips to help you along your way.

Cook's Assistant Quest

Difficulty level: Very easy
Requirements: None

Location of quest:
Town of Lumbridge, in the castle.
Who are you doing the quest for?
The castle cook.
How do you begin this quest? Find the cook in the castle's kitchen and talk to him. He will tell you his story and then you can offer to help him or not. If you offer to help him, your quest will begin!
Object of the quest: The cook needs to bake a cake for the duke's birthday, but he is out of ingredients. He wants you to get the ingredients for him: some milk, an egg, and some flour.

Be sure to have: A bucket and a pot.
Reward: You are awarded 1 quest point (QP) and 300 cooking XP. If you keep talking to the cook after completing the quest, he will let you use the castle's stove so you can cook your own food. Take him up on it – a stove lets you cook your food without burning it so easily.
Tip: Don't forget to use your map! It will help you figure out where you need to go.

Hint: *The windmill has three levels.*

Romeo & Juliet

Difficulty level: Very easy
Requirements: None

Location of quest:
Juliet's house in Varrock.
Who are you doing the quest for?
Juliet and Romeo.
How do you begin this quest? Find Juliet in her house in northwest Varrock.
Object of the quest: Juliet wants you to give a message to Romeo. Juliet's father doesn't approve of their relationship and they want to run away together. First you must deliver a message from Juliet to Romeo, then make a potion to give to Juliet which will help them to run away.

Reward: 5 QPs
Tip: All NPCs appear as yellow dots on your map screen. If you can't find Romeo in the crowded town square, walk in the direction of the yellow dot.

Hint: *Cadava berries can be found in the woods.*

Sheep Shearer

Difficulty level: Very easy
Requirements: None

Location of quest: Northwest of Lumbridge, in the house next to the chicken coop.
Who are you doing the quest for?
Fred the farmer.
How do you begin this quest? Go to the house next to the chicken coop. Talk to Fred, whom you'll find either inside or outside of the house.
Object of the quest: Fred the farmer needs help shearing his sheep. He wants you to shear some sheep and bring him back 20 balls of wool.

Be sure to get: One pair of shears, which cost 1 GP at the general store.
Reward: 1 QP, 150 crafting XP, and 60 GPs
Tip: If a sheep runs away while you're trying to shear it, don't give up! You'll get it eventually.

Doric's Quest

Difficulty level: Easy
Requirements: None, but it's easier to do with a higher mining XP

Location of quest:
In a house north of Falador.
Who are you doing the quest for?
Doric the dwarf.
How do you begin this quest?
Speak to Doric in his house and ask if you can use his anvils.
Object of the quest:
Doric will let you use his anvils on one condition: if you get him 6 clay, 4 copper ores, and 2 iron ores.
Be sure to have: A mining tool, such as a pickaxe.

Reward: You are awarded 1 QP, 1,300 mining XP, 180 GPs, and use of Doric's anvil.
Tip: It's easy to get lost in the mines, so remember where you entered!

Hint: *If you can't mine the iron, check out the store in the mine.*

Goblin Diplomacy

Difficulty level: Easy
Requirements: None

Location of quest:
Rusty Anchor Bar in Port Sarim.
Who are you doing the quest for?
The bartender.
How do you begin this quest? Talk to the bartender at the Rusty Anchor.
Object of the quest: Business has been bad at the bar, because the threat of a goblin war has scared away the customers. The goblins have been arguing about what color their armor should be. You need to help the goblin generals decide on an armor color.

Be sure to have: About 50 GPs, on you, so you can purchase the things you need.
Reward: 5 QP, 200 crafting XP, and a gold bar
Tip: An easy way to get goblin mail is to kill a goblin in the village.

Hint: *Goblin generals are hard to please! Having a backup choice will save you time.*

Imp Catcher

Difficulty level: Easy
Requirements: None

Location of start of quest:
The Wizard's Tower.
Who are you doing the quest for?
Wizard Mizgog.
How do you begin this quest? Talk to
Wizard Mizgog, who is in the attic of the
Wizard's Tower. You must say please
when you ask him for a quest.
Object of the quest:
Imps have stolen some of Mizgog's
magical beads: red, yellow, black,
and white. He wants you to return the
beads to him.

Reward: 1 QP, 875 magic XP, and an amulet of accuracy
Tip: You will find lots of imps at the volcano on Karamja.

The Restless Ghost

Difficulty level: Easy
Requirements: The ability to defeat a level 13 Skeleton is helpful.

Location of start of quest:
Town of Lumbridge, in the church.
Who are you doing the quest for?
Father Aereck.
How do you begin this quest? Go to the
church and talk to Father Aereck. Ask him
if he has a quest for you.
Object of the quest:
Father Aereck has a ghost that is
disturbing the peace in the church
graveyard. He wants you to put the
ghost to rest. His friend Father Urhney
can help you.

Reward: 1 QP, 1,125 prayer XP, and the amulet of ghostspeak
Tip: If you can't defeat a level 13 Skeleton when you try this quest, run for your life when
you see it!

Hint: *Look for the skull in the northeast room of the church basement.*

Rune Mysteries

Difficulty level: Easy
Requirements: None

Location of start of quest:
Town of Lumbridge, in the castle.
Who are you doing the quest for?
Duke Horacio.
How do you begin this quest? Find Duke Horacio upstairs in the castle. Ask him if he has any quests.
Object of the quest: The duke has found a mysterious object, the Air talisman, and wants a Wizard named Sedridor to examine it. After you bring the Air talisman to Sedridor, the Wizard will ask you to bring a research package to Aurbury the rune-seller in return for some research notes.
Reward: 1 QP, access to the Rune essence mine, and access to the Air talisman
Tip: Aurbury's rune shop is marked on the map with a Fire symbol.

Witch's Potion

Difficulty level: Easy
Requirements: None

Location of quest:
In Hetty's house in Rimmington.
Who are you doing the quest for?
Hetty the witch.
How do you begin this quest? Visit Hetty the witch and ask her for a quest. When she questions you, answer yes.
Object of the quest: To get some potion ingredients for Hetty: eye of newt, a rat's tail, an onion, and a burnt piece of meat.
Reward: 1 QP and 325 magic XP
Tip: You won't have to go far from Rimmington to get the ingredients you need.

The Wilderness

rthorpe

ero's
Guild   Chaos Temple   Black
                     Goblin   Ca   Knight's
                     Village   Edgeville
Druid's
Circle   Lumber
                                                                                          Yard
erly   Palace

                Ice Mountain   Yarrock
                        Dwarven   Cook's
                         Mine   Guild   Dig Site
                     Barbarian
                      Village
                                                                                                    Exam
        Falador   Centre
     White   Draynor
ard's Knight's   Manor
     Castle

                                Draynor
Port Sarim
elzar's   Duel
ze   Lumbridge   Arena
nington

                        Wizard's   Al-Kharid
                        Tower

                                                                        Shantay
                                                                         Pass

RUNE
SCAPE

Black Knights' Fortress

Difficulty level: Medium
Requirements: 12 QP and the ability to defeat level 33 Black Knights.

Location of quest:
In the second floor of the White Knights' Castle in Falador.
Who are you doing the quest for?
The White Knights.
How do you begin this quest?
Talk to Sir Amik Varze on the third floor of the castle.
Object of the quest: The Black Knights are up to no good. The White Knights want you to spy on them and uncover their evil scheme.
Reward: 3 QPs and 2,500 GPs

Tip: A disguise can help you sneak into the Black Knights' Fortress.

Hint: *A cabbage can save the day!*

Ernest the Chicken

Difficulty level: Medium
Requirements: None

Location of quest: Outside of Draynor Manor, in northern Draynor Village.
Who are you doing the quest for?
Veronica.
How do you begin this quest? Speak to Veronica outside of Draynor Manor.
Object of the quest: Veronica and her fiancé, Ernest, were lost. Ernest went inside the spooky-looking manor to ask for directions, but he never came out. You must agree to go into the manor to find Ernest. When you enter, you'll find out he's been turned into a chicken by Professor Oddenstein. You need to help the professor turn Ernest back into a human by gathering three things for his machine: a pressure gauge, a rubber tube, and an oil can.
Reward: 4 QPs and 300 GPs
Tip: Pick up any interesting items you find in the mansion. They may help you get the items you need.

Hint: *There is a secret door in the mansion!*

Pirate's Treasure

Difficulty level: Medium
Requirements: None

Location of quest: Port Sarim, on the dock behind the Rusty Anchor Bar.
Who are you doing the quest for?
Redbeard Frank.
How do you begin this quest?
Talk to Redbeard Frank and ask him about treasure.
Object of the quest:
Redbeard Frank will tell you where to find One-Eyed Hector's pirate treasure if you get him a bottle of Karamja Rum. Bring the rum back to Frank, and follow the clues to the pirate's treasure.

Be sure to have: About 90 GPs and a spade.
Reward: 2 QPs and the treasure
Tip: White aprons are sold in the Varrock clothes shop for 2 GPs.

Hint: *Banana crates are excellent for smuggling items through customs.*

Prince Ali Rescue

Difficulty level: Medium
Requirements: None

Location of quest: Al-Kharid, in the castle.
Who are you doing the quest for?
Hassan and Osman.
How do you begin this quest? Find Hassan in the castle in Al-Kharid and ask him if he needs help. He does want your help, but he wants you to talk to Osman, who can be found outside the castle.
Object of the quest: Osman tells you that Prince Ali has been kidnapped by Lady Keli, and is being held hostage in the jail near Draynor Village. Hassan and Osman want you to attempt a dangerous rescue.

You must put together a disguise to smuggle Prince Ali out of the jail. Break into the jail, and flee with the disguised prince.
Reward: 3 QPs and 700 GPs. You also become an official friend of Al-Kharid, and can pass through the toll gates for free from now on!

Tip: The Jail Guards will attack anyone who comes near the jail. You can fight these level 26 guards, or wait until they are off harassing other players before you approach Lady Keli.

Hint: *A shop in Varrock sells a pink shirt just like Lady Keli's.*

Demon Slayer

Difficulty level: Difficult
Requirements: You should be able to defeat an apocalyptic demon.

Location of quest: Varrock Square, next to the clothing shop and west of the Varrock fountain.
Who are you doing the quest for?
The Gypsy.
How do you begin this quest? When the Gypsy asks if she can read your future, say yes!
Object of the quest: A mighty demon has been summoned to destroy the city of Varrock. The Gypsy tells you that you are the one destined to stop him!

Reward: 3 QPs and the silverlight sword
Tip: Killing chickens is a quick way to get the bones you will need for this quest.

Shield of Arrav

Difficulty level: Novice
Requirements: One friend who has not started the quest yet

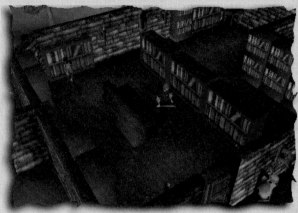

Location of quest: In Varrock Castle, in the library (the northernmost room).
Who are you doing the quest for?
Reldo the librarian.
How do you begin this quest? You and your friend both should visit Reldo and ask him if he has a quest for you.
Object of the quest: A valuable shield has been stolen from the museum of Varrock by a gang of professional thieves. You and your friend will have to go undercover to try to track down the shield and return it to the museum.

Be sure to have: 20 GPs
Reward: 1 QP and 600 GPs
Tip: The friend with the highest combat XP should join the Phoenix gang of thieves.

Vampire Slayer

Difficulty level: Difficult
Requirements: You should be able to defeat a vampire.

Location of quest:
In Morgan's house in Draynor Village.
Who are you doing the quest for?
A villager named Morgan.
How do you begin this quest?
Find Morgan's house in the center of the village and talk to him. Tell him you will help him with his problem.
Object of the quest:
A vampire is terrorizing the people of Draynor Village. Morgan will send you to Dr. Harlow, who will tell you how to slay the vampire. Be sure to have: some food with you, to restore hit points while you are fighting.
Be sure to have: One pair of shears, which cost 1 GP at the general store
Reward: 3 QPs and 4,825 attack XP
Tip: If you don't want to end up as vampire food, don't attempt this quest unless you have a high overall combat XP!

Hint: *Morgan has some garlic in his house.*

The Knight's Sword

Difficulty level: Intermediate
Requirements: Mining level of 10 or above; must not be afraid of level 57 Ice Warriors

Location of quest: In the courtyard of the White Knights' Castle in Falador.
Who are you doing the quest for? Sir Vyvin's squire.
How do you begin this quest? You can usually find the squire in the castle gardens. Ask him how he's doing, and he'll tell you his troubles. Offer to help him to begin your quest.
Object of the quest: Sir Vyvin's squire has lost his master's sword. You need to find one of the Imcando Dwarves to help you make a new sword.
Reward: 1 QP and 12,725 smithing XP

Tip: The dwarf swordmaker will make an extra sword for you if you have extra materials and ask nicely!

Hint: *The portrait of the sword can be found inside a cupboard.*

Dragon Slayer

Difficulty level: Most difficult; an experienced quest
Requirements: You must be a member of the Champion's Guild and have the ability to kill a level 83 Dragon!

Location of quest: The Champion's Guild, which is located southwest of Varrock's south exit. To enter you need at least 32 QPs.
Who are you doing the quest for? Oziach, a friend of the Guild Master.
How do you begin this quest? Find the Guild Master and ask him about rune platemail. He will send you to his friend Oziach. Ask him how to prove you're a hero.
Object of the quest: Oziach will tell you to kill Elvarg the Dragon on Crandor Isle.
Reward: 2 QPs; the ability to wear Rune Platemail and Dragon Leather, and lots and lots of extra combat XP!

Tip: Bring some high-energy food with you so you can restore hit points during the fierce battle with Elvarg.

Hint: *You can buy a Wizard Mind Bomb at the pub in Falador.*

Characters and Creatures

There are so many people in RuneScape to meet! So many creatures to battle! This section will give you some info about each of them so you'll know what to do when you encounter one.

Air Wizard

Height: 5 ft. 8 in.
Weight: 160 lbs.
Varieties: Level 13
Locations: North of the Rimmington mine
Appearance: Solid enough to fight
Description: A practiced Mage who specializes in the Air spells. His skills with Air magic give him the ability to heal if Air spells are used against him.
When you see one, you should: Pretty much anything except an Air spell will work.

Bandit

Height: 5 ft. 11 in.
Weight: 235 lbs.
Varieties: Level 21
Locations: The Wilderness
Appearance: Human
Description: They live by the Bandits' code: Steal from the rich and give to the poor. Of course, to bandits, they're the "poor," and the "rich" are everyone else.
When you see one, you should: Stay away if you're not at a high enough level to defeat him, unless you feel like losing your gold. Otherwise, go ahead and attack. You just might be able to rob the robber.

Barbarian

Height: 6 ft. 2 in.
Weight: 235 lbs.
Varieties: Levels 10, 15, and 17
Locations: The Barbarian Village
Appearance: Warriors with big muscles, beards, and rustic armor
Description: Barbarians used to roam RuneScape, although they've settled down in recent years. They don't usually take sides in the battles of good versus evil that go on in RuneScape.
When you see one, you should: Use magic if you can when you battle.

Barbarian Woman

Height: 5 ft. 9 in.
Weight: 160 lbs.
Varieties: Levels 9 and 10
Locations: The Barbarian Village
Appearance: Muscle-clad female warriors
Description: Self-sufficient, having plundered and pillaged in the tribal warfare of days past. Some contemporary Barbarians have now dropped anchor with settlements of their own. Remaining relatively neutral, they could be a useful force indeed if anyone could tempt them into alliance. . . .
When you see one, you should: Attack to get combat XP, but don't underestimate this warrior – Barbarian Women can be even tougher than men!

Bear

Height: 5 ft. (8 ft. at full stretch)
Weight: 600 lbs.
Varieties: Levels 19 and 21
Locations: You'll find Bears roaming in the forests.
Appearance: Large and furry
Description: Don't mistake these big beasts for teddy bears! Hunters will often seek them for their fur, but these powerful animals can defend themselves pretty well.
When you see one, you should: Try not to disturb it.

Black Knight

Height: 6 ft.
Weight: 200 lbs.
Varieties: Level 33
Locations: Black Knight Fortress in the north and the Lava Maze (in the Wilderness)
Appearance: Those 200 pounds are all muscle.
Description: These black-clad knights are fierce in battle and known for their villainous behavior. But they also have a love for the finer things in life, like poetry and fine food.
When you see one, you should: Show some respect, unless you want to get pummeled.

Chaos Dwarf

Height: 4 ft. 3 in.
Weight: 220 lbs.
Varieties: Level 48
Locations: In the Wilderness
Appearance: These hefty dwarves have a reddish hue to their skin. Some say it's because they're constantly angry and ready to fight.
Description: These hotheaded dwarves would rather slam an axe in your face than shake your hand.
When you see one, you should: Get ready for a battle you'll never forget! (if you have enough combat XP)

Chicken

Height: 12 in.
Weight: 5 lbs.
Varieties: Level 1
Locations: Chicken pens, in Lumbridge and around RuneScape
Appearance: Mouthwatering
Description: Chickens are fast walkers, probably because beginners love to prey on chickens to up their levels.
When you see one, you should: Kill it for its meat and feathers.

Cow

Height: 5 ft. 10 in.
Weight: 1,500 lbs.
Varieties: Level 2
Locations: Enclosures north of Lumbridge, and near the crafting guild
Appearance: Beefy
Description: These animals are an important source of food and leather in RuneScape.
When you see one, you should: Milk it if it's a dairy cow, and if it's a beef cow, slaughter it for its meat and cowhide.

Dark Warrior

Height: 5 ft. 10 in.
Weight: 200 lbs.
Varieties: Level 8
Locations: The Wilderness
Appearance: Well armed
Description: These warriors are motivated by money. They like to hang around with other shady characters.
When you see one, you should: Leave them alone, unless you're looking for trouble. Dark Warriors don't like to be bothered.

Dark Wizard

Height: 5 ft. 8 in.
Weight: 160 lbs.
Varieties: Levels 7 and 20
Locations: The Stone Circle south of Varrock, the Wilderness, and the fishing spot in Draynor village
Appearance: Like a Wizard, only darker
Description: These treacherous mages have been known to turn on each other. They can't be trusted. Level 7 Dark Wizards like to attack players at random.
When you see one, you should: Battle it if you have enough combat XP.

Dwarf

Height: 4 ft. 2 in.
Weight: 200 lbs.
Varieties: Level 10
Locations: In and around the Ice Mountain and the Dwarven Mine.
Appearance: Short and stout
Description: Dwarves are not happy unless they are mining iron ore – and even then, they're not really that happy.
When you see one, you should: Battle it to raise your XP level.

Farmer

Height: 5 ft. 10 in.
Weight: 180 lbs.
Varieties: Level 7
Locations: On farms and near windmills throughout RuneScape
Description: These hardworking folk can be surprisingly wealthy. It is rumored that some farmers hoard valuable rune-stones.
When you see one, you should: Talk to him, unless he's angry with you for trespassing on his land.

Fire Wizard

Height: 5 ft. 8 in.
Weight: 160 lbs.
Varieties: Level 13
Locations: North of the Rimmington mine
Appearance: Fiery
Description: A practiced Mage who specializes in the Fire spells. His skills with Fire magic give him the ability to heal if Fire spells are used against him.
When you see one, you should: Don't bother trying a Fire spell against him.

Ghost

Height: How can you measure a ghost?
Weight: You can't weigh a spirit!
Varieties: Levels 19 and 24
Locations: Draynor Manor and Varrock sewers' dungeon
Appearance: Otherworldly
Description: Ghosts aren't too happy to be stuck between the worlds of the living and the dead.
When you see one, you should: Try not to disturb it, or it will attack.

Giant

Height: 7 ft. 2 in.
Weight: 290 lbs.
Varieties: Levels 28 (hill) and 42 (moss)
Locations: The Wilderness and most dungeons
Appearance: Really, really tall
Description: Giants are said to be one of the oldest races in RuneScape. They like to keep to themselves and will attack anyone who gets under their feet.
When you see one, you should: Wish you were bigger!

Giant Rat

Height: 2 ft.
Weight: 120 lbs.
Varieties: Levels 3 and 6
Locations: Lumbridge swamp, Varrock slums and sewers, and dungeons around RuneScape
Appearance: Dirty gray with beady eyes
Description: They slink around filthy places, eating from rotting carcasses.
When you see one, you should: Kill it.

King Scorpion

Height: Up to 6 ft. long
Weight: Up to 240 lbs.
Varieties: Level 32
Locations: Dwarven Mines
Appearance: They look like extremely aggressive lobsters.
Description: Some creatures will attack only when you bother them, but not King Scorpions. If you just walk past one, it will attack you! So run first, and ask questions later!
When you see one, you should: Run away if you don't have a high combat level.

Giant Spider

Height: 30 ft.
Weight: 20 lbs.
Varieties: Levels 2 and 27
Locations: You'll find them hanging out in the Lumbridge Castle basement, and in sewers and houses.
Appearance: Eight-legged and scary
Description: They may bite you if you're not careful where you're walking and bump into one. Otherwise, they'll often vanish down giant plugholes.
When you see one, you should: Attack it – if it's level 2, that is.

Goblin

Height: 5 ft. 4 in.
Weight: 180 lbs.
Varieties: Levels 2, 5, and 13 (with spear)
Locations: All over RuneScape, especially Lumbridge and the woods near Port Sarim
Appearance: Green and warty
Description: They're weak, and not too brave or smart. They are good targets for low-level players.
When you see one, you should: Attack if you want to raise your combat XP and gain some money or items to boot.

Greater Demon

Height: 8 ft. 6 in.
Weight: 350 lbs.
Varieties: Level 92
Locations: In the ruins in the northeast Wilderness
Appearance: Horned, winged, and dangerous!
Description: These beasts are cruel killing machines.
When you see one, you should: Wish you were someplace else! A Greater Demon can kill you in a matter of seconds.

Guard

Height: 5 ft. 10 in.
Weight: 220 lbs.
Varieties: Levels 21 and 22
Locations: Wherever things need guarding, especially banks and gates in the towns
Appearance: Stocky and not very friendly-looking
Description: These tough guys take their jobs seriously. If they're not supposed to let someone pass, they won't. But if they see a crime happening down the street, they'll look the other way.
When you see one, you should: Wait until he is distracted, then try to sneak past him.

Guard Bandits

Height: 5 ft. 11 in.
Weight: Up to 70 lbs.
Varieties: Level 22
Locations: The Wilderness
Appearance: Human
Description: They make it tougher to get into their Bandit camp by attacking people passing through the entrance.
When you see one, you should: Watch out – especially if you're trying to get into their camp!

Highwayman

Height: 6 ft.
Weight: 200 lbs.
Varieties: Level 5
Locations: At major crossroads, south of Draynor Manor, and between Rimmington and Falador
Appearance: Stylish human wearing a cape and sometimes a mask
Description: Like a robber with fashion sense. But don't be fooled by his dashing demeanor. Highwaymen love to jump out at unsuspecting travelers and tourists and attack them and steal their money. You'll know them by their signature cry: "Stand and deliver!"
When you see one, you should: Fight back! If you're a low-level player, a Highwayman can do a lot of damage.

Hobgoblin

Height: 5 ft. 8 in.
Weight: 200 lbs.
Varieties: Levels 28 and 42 (with spear)
Locations: The Wilderness dungeons and the peninsula behind the crafting guild
Appearance: Larger and stronger than regular goblins, but not as smart – if you can believe that!
Description: They like to keep their teeth sharp so they can eat their opponents.
When you see one, you should: Be wary. Sometimes Hobgoblins attack, and sometimes they don't.

Ice Giant

Height: 7 ft. 2 in.
Weight: 290 lbs.
Varieties: Level 53
Locations: Dungeon near Thurgo's house; the Wilderness
Appearance: Tall and frigid!
Description: One of the oldest races in RuneScape, Ice Giants have evolved to adapt to the environment and can survive and fight very well in cold and icy conditions.
When you see one, you should: Give them plenty of space and try to avoid getting under their feet – unless of course you have a high enough combat level to take them on!

Ice Warrior

Height: Varies
Weight: Unknown
Varieties: Level 57
Locations: Ice Giant's Cave and the Wilderness
Appearance: They look like human men but are made of ice.
Description: These mysterious men can be dangerous when disturbed.
When you see one, you should: Be very, very polite. Ice Warriors can't stand players with attitude.

Imp

Height: 10 in.
Weight: 15 lbs.
Varieties: Level 2
Locations: Imps have an annoying habit of turning up everywhere!
Appearance: Small and bright red
Description: These little devils use their small size to their advantage: They love to steal little items such as wool, beads, food, and hats.
When you see one, you should: Act quickly! Imps will run away just as you're about to slay them.

Jail Guard

Height: 5 ft. 9 in.
Weight: 210 lbs.
Varieties: Level 26
Locations: East of Draynor Village
Appearance: Greasy and sloppy. They're technically human, but they barely make the cut.
Description: Just plain rotten. They love to torment their prisoners, and they will attack anyone who goes near the jail, even if they're just walking by!
When you see one, you should: Run away. If you really need to get into the jail, wait until they are distracted and sneak past.

Lesser Demon

Height: 8 ft. 3 in.
Weight: 320 lbs.
Varieties: Level 82
Locations: Karamja, Melzar's Maze, Lava Maze, Wizard's Tower, and Crandor
Appearance: Red with large horns
Description: They might be called "Lesser" Demons, but they've got fiery tempers and are just as dangerous as other demons.
When you see one, you should: Run away – unless you're a particularly tough adventurer. Or you could try slowly killing the caged one in the Wizard's Tower.

Man

Height: 5 ft. 10 in.
Weight: 175 lbs.
Varieties: Level 2 (generic man)
Locations: Everywhere
Description: Humans are the most numerous species in RuneScape. They're constantly being attacked by players trying to increase their levels.
When you see one, you should: Do what your conscience tells you to. Some players like the easy combat experience. Others prefer not to attack fellow humans, and talk to them instead.

Monk

Height: 6 ft.
Weight: 180 lbs.
Varieties: Levels 3 and 5
Locations: The monastery west of Edgeville
Appearance: Human, wearing robes
Description: These men lead peaceful lives of prayer and devotion.
When you see one, you should: Be nice! Monks will heal you if you are injured.

Monk of Zamorak

Height: 6 ft.
Weight: 180 lbs.
Varieties: Level 22
Locations: Chaos Temple of north Asgarnia
Appearance: These monks adorn themselves with the blood-red robes of Zamorak.
Description: Zamorak is the ultra-evil dude who threatens all of RuneScape. His monks worship him and do his bidding. They're not so nice.
When you see one, you should: Battle at your own risk.

Mugger

Height: 5 ft. 10 in.
Weight: 160 lbs.
Varieties: Level 6
Locations: Varrock Castle
Appearance: Shifty-looking
Description: A mugger is as dashing as a Highwayman, but he's more violent than a Thief. All three of them want to steal from you, and the Mugger will definitely harm you in the process.
When you see one, you should: Fight back. You can probably take him.

Pirate

Height: 5 ft. 9 in.
Weight: 215 lbs.
Varieties: Levels 19, 20 and 25
Locations: Port Sarim, Karamja Island, and sometimes the Ice Giant cave
Appearance: You can usually recognize a pirate by the eye patch he's wearing.
Description: These merry men love eating and having fun – especially when they're spending your money!
When you see one, you should: Hang out and have a good time – but keep an eye on your GPs!

Rat

Height: Up to 5 ft.
Weight: Up to 70 lbs.
Varieties: Levels 1 and 3
Locations: Most sewers and many dungeons
Appearance: Mouselike
Description: Living in sewers and underground areas, Rats are a fairly common type of pest littered across RuneScape.
When you see one, you should: Attack it, especially if you need a rat's tail.

Scorpion

Height: up to 3 ft. long
Weight: up to 120 lbs.
Varieties: Level 12
Locations: Dwarven Mines
Appearance: Like big, punk-rock lobsters
Description: A Scorpion will sting you with its tail. Ouch!
When you see one, you should: Either ignore it or, if your combat level is high enough, fight it.

Sheep

Height: 3 ft. 6 in.
Weight: 230 lbs.
Varieties: Level 0
Locations: The sheep farm near Lumbridge
Appearance: Moving balls of fluff
Description: Sheep are peaceful and passive.
When you see one, you should: Shear it to get its wool.

Skeleton

Height: Varies, depending on the previous owner of the bones
Weight: About 100 lbs., or more for "big-boned" skeletons
Varieties: Various levels
Locations: Wizard's Tower, Draynor Manor, Varrock sewers, and Edgeville Dungeon
Appearance: Skinny
Description: These soldiers of the dead love violence. Higher-level Skeletons tend to be more aggressive.
When you see one, you should: Fight or run, depending on your combat XP.

Spider

Height: Up to 10 in.
Weight: Up to 20 lbs.
Varieties: Levels 1 and 2
Locations: Most sewers and many dungeons
Appearance: Creepy
Description: Living in sewers and underground areas, Spiders are a fairly common type of monster littered across RuneScape.
When you see one, you should: Attack it to gain combat XP.

Thief

Height: 5 ft. 9 in.
Weight: 180 lbs.
Varieties: Level 16
Locations: Skulking around Varrock
Appearance: Human
Description: They like hanging out with pirates and comparing loot.
When you see one, you should: While they won't normally attack you, they will definitely fight back if you attack them, and they're fairly strong.

Unicorn

Height: 5 ft. 6 in.
Weight: 260 lbs.
Varieties: Level 15
Locations: The woods south of Varrock and south of Edgeville
Appearance: Like a horse with a horn
Description: These peaceful creatures may have magical abilities, but no one is sure what they are. They definitely have a soothing effect on people who go near them.
When you see one, you should: Behold the wonder of this amazing creature.

Water Wizard

Height: 5 ft. 8 in.
Weight: 160 lbs.
Varieties: Level 13
Locations: North of the Rimmington mine
Appearance: Hydro-powered
Description: A practiced Mage who specializes in Water spells, he is able to heal himself if one is used against him.
When you see one, you should: Use anything but a Water spell against him.

White Knight

Height: 5 ft. 11 in.
Weight: 195 lbs.
Varieties: Level 36
Locations: The White Knights have their own castle in Falador.
Appearance: Striking knights in shiny armor
Description: White Knights have a reputation for being the goody-two-shoes of RuneScape. Maybe it's because they're so polite. Still, you have to admire them for their dedication to the forces of good, and for their unfailing sense of honor.
When you see one, you should: Be polite back, as they can be fearsome warriors.

Witch

Height: 5 ft. 4 in.
Weight: 150 lbs.
Varieties: Level 25
Locations: South Kharid and Draynor Manor
Appearance: You can usually tell a witch by her pointy hat.
Description: These wise women practice the useful magical crafts of old RuneScape. They tend to be loners because their powers are distrusted by others.
When you see one, you should: Be nice! She may be able to do something helpful for you.

Wizard

Height: 5 ft. 8 in.
Weight: 160 lbs.
Varieties: Level 9
Locations: The Wizard's Tower
Appearance: Long robes and pointy hats
Description: The Wizards hold a special place in RuneScape history. But when they joined with the Dark Wizards, they plunged the land into chaos. They are very protective of the runestones, which are becoming harder and harder to find.
When you see one, you should: See what you can learn, if you want to master the skill of magic.

Woman

Height: 5 ft. 8 in.
Weight: 160 lbs.
Varieties: Level 2
Locations: Like Men, they can be found all over RuneScape.
Appearance: Human, but prettier than Men
Description: Humans are certainly quite advanced creatures, building large communities and various labor-saving devices.
When you see one, you should: Either attack or not attack. The choice is up to you.

Zombie

Height: 5 ft. 6 in.
Weight: 180 lbs.
Varieties: Various levels
Locations: Varrock sewers and other hidden locations
Description: These terrifying creatures crave flesh and will attack any living thing that dares to come near them.
When you see one, you should: Hold your nose! Nothing smells worse than a living corpse. Oh, and you should probably run, too – fast!

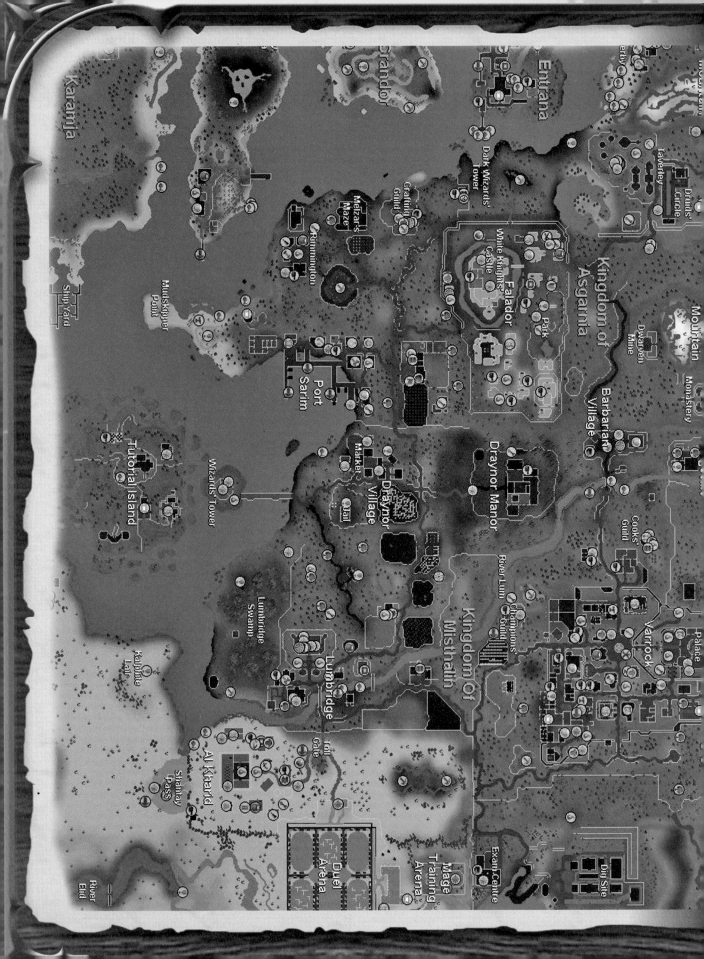

Ice path

Maps

White Wolf Mountain

Troll Stronghold

Death Plateau

Trollheim

Burthorpe

Heroes Guild

Chaos Temple

Druids' Circle

Goblin Village

Ice Mountain

Black Knights' Fortress

Monastery

Edgeville

Ruins

The Forgotten Cemetery

Dark Knight Fortress

Bandit Camp

Lava Maze

Wilderness

Graveyard of Shadows

Ruins

Red Dragon Isle

White Knights' Palace

Chaos Temple

Bone Yard

Demonic Ruins

Lumber Yard

RuneScape is filled with exciting places to explore. The maps and information on these pages will help you navigate the world more easily.

About Lumbridge

You will start your RuneScape adventure in Lumbridge. It's not the best place to find shops, but it's rich in farms, fish, and goblins to battle. You can pick cabbage, potatoes, and wheat, and even kill chickens and cows to eat for free. When your belly is filled with all that free food, go battle some low-level monsters or characters to build up your overall combat XP.

Places to Shop

Bob's Brilliant Axes sells axes and battle-axes; he also repairs them if they break.
Lumbridge General Store

Places of Interest

Lumbridge Castle, where you may find the start of a few quests

People of Interest

The Lumbridge Guide has lots of helpful info for you.
Gee and Donie can also give you some tips.

Also Look For...

Cabbage farm, for free veggies (so what if they don't taste great?)
Chicken coop, for free chicken, feathers, and eggs
Church with altar, to recharge your prayer points
Cooking ranges, essential for baking things like bread and pies
Cow farm, with beef or cowhide for the taking
Fishing
Furnace, for smelting ore
Onion farm, for free onions to spice up your cooking
Potato farm, for yummy free spuds
Sheep farm, where you can find free wool
Spinning wheel, for spinning wool
Water, for cooking and crafting
Windmill, to turn wheat into grain

River Lum

Champions'
Guild

Kingdom Of
Misthalin

Lumbridge

Toll
Gate

Lumbridge
Swamp

Al Kharid

Shantay
Pass

Kalphite
Lair

About Al-Kharid

This city is east of Lumbridge. You must pay 10 GPs to enter the city through the toll-gate, but if you want to save your gold, you can take a long journey around the border fence. (Once you complete the Prince Ali Rescue quest, however, you can pass through the gates for free.) In this exotic desert land, you will find unique items to buy, fascinating people, and camels.

Places to Shop

Al-Kharid General Store, for nearly everything under the desert sun
Dommick's Crafting Store, which sells crafting supplies
Gem Stall
Karim's Kebab Store, for tasty desert cuisine
Louie's Armored Legs, for your leg-plate needs
Ranael's Super Skirt Store, for plate skirts for battle
Silk Stall
Zeke's Superior Scimitars

Places of Interest

Al-Kharid Castle, where Prince Ali's Rescue begins

People of Interest

Ellis the tanner will tan your cowhides for you.

Also Look For . . .

Bank
Cooking ranges
Furnace
Mining
Water

Lumbridge

Toll
Gate

Duel
Arena

mbridge
vamp

Al Kharid

Shantay
Pass

Here be

Kalphite
Lair

River
Elid

About Varrock

The largest city in RuneScape is almost always very crowded. That's probably because it's so convenient to find what you need. It's loaded with shops, mysterious places, and two banks. Be careful when you visit this city, though. To the north is the Wilderness where the action is no-holds-barred and other players are able to kill you. If you are a new player, be wary if someone tells you to follow them into the Wilderness.

Places to Shop

Apothecary
Aubury's Rune Shop
Bareak the fur trader
Blue Moon Inn
Dancing Donkey Bar
Horvick's Armor Shop
Jolly Boar Inn
Lowe's Archery Emporium
Varrock Swordshop
Thessalia Fine Clothes
Zaff's Superior Staffs

Places of Interest

Varrock Church, where you can recharge your prayer
Varrock Palace
Stone Circle, where Dark Wizards like to gather

People of Interest

Romeo and Juliet, who will send you on a quest
Reldo, the librarian who can be found in Varrock Castle
The gypsy will ask to read your fortune to you.

Also Look For . . .

Anvil
Banks
Cooking ranges
Field of cadava and redberries
Furnace
Water

Lumber Yard

Palace

ville

Cooks'
Guild

Varrock

nor Manor

River Lum

Champions'
Guild

Kingdom Of
Misthalin

About Falador

This city is located in central RuneScape. It's a nice place to visit, with lots of statues and a big park with beautiful gardens. After you see the sights, you can browse for some battle gear in one of Falador's shops.

Places to Shop

Cassie's Shield Shop
Falador General Store
Flynn's Mace Market
Herquin's Gems
Wayne's Chains! Chainmail Specialist

People of Interest

Hairdresser
Visit the makeover mage to completely change your character's appearance – for a 3,000 GP fee!
Wyson the Gardener takes care of Falador's beautiful gardens.

Also Look For . . .

Anvils
Bank
Barbershop
Cooking ranges
Furnace
Water

Here's a hint for all questers:
Falador plays an important role
in the Pirate's Treasure quest.

Dwarven
Mine

**Barbarian
Village**

Kingdom of
Asgarnia

Park

E

Falador

White Knights'
Castle

Wizards'
wer

D

**Crafting
Guild**

**Melzar's
Maze**

Mar

About Draynor Village

When you are just starting out, Draynor Village is the place to go to fish for food. Here, fishermen with the lowest XP can cast their nets and build up fishing XP. You won't find too many places to shop in this country town, but you will find many people who can do things for you.

Places to Shop

Diango Toy Store, although it's more a cart than a real shop
Diango can return holiday items if you've lost them

People of Interest

Aggie the Witch, a dye maker
Ned, a sailor and master rope maker

Also Look For . . .

Bank
Fishing spot
Jail
Wheat farm

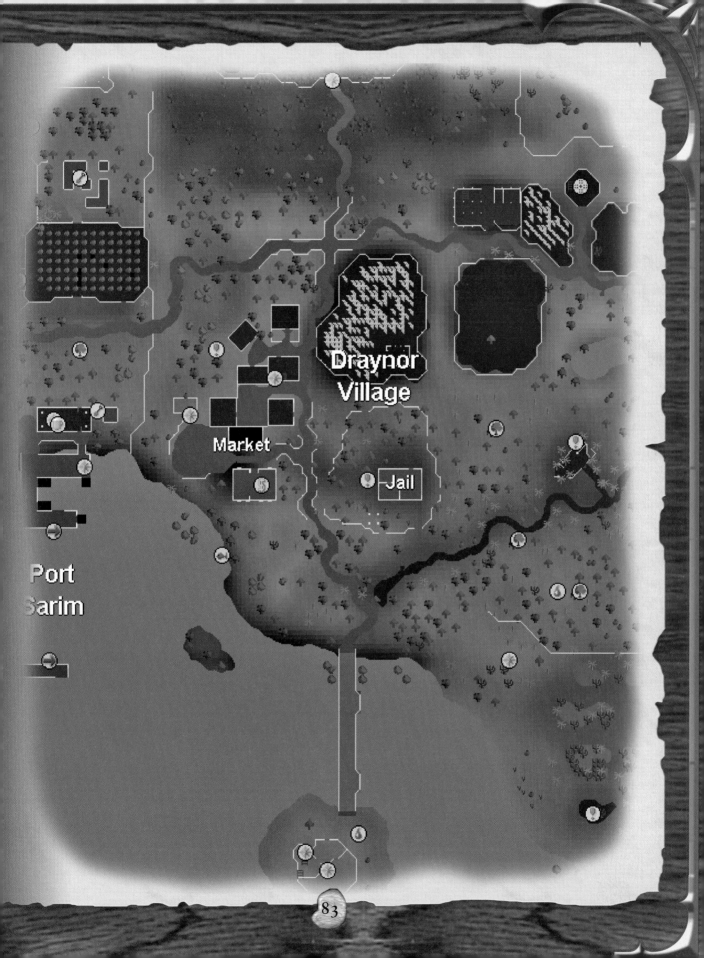

Draynor Village

Market

Jail

Port Sarim

About Port Sarim

This charming little sea town is located near Draynor Village. Once you build up your fishing XP, Port Sarim is the place to go. You can buy all kinds of fishing equipment here. Some visitors may stay away from Port Sarim because of its pirate inhabitants, but they're generally too busy having a good time to hassle anyone.

Places to Shop

Betty's Magic Emporium, where you can find all kinds of runes
Brian's Axes
Gerrant's Fishing Business, where you can buy equipment and sell what you catch
Grum's Gold Exchange, a seller of gold jewelry
Rusty Anchor Bar
Wydin's Grocery Store, a great place for cooks to shop

People of Interest

Redbeard Frank, a pirate who may send you on a quest if you ask . . .

Also Look For . . .

Anvil
Cooking range
Church (with altar)
Dock, where you can catch a boat
to Karamja Island
Fishing
Jail

Market

Port
Sarim

on

Wizar

Mudskipper

About Karamja Island

After you buy fishing equipment at Port Sarim, pay 30 GPs for a boat ride to Karamja Island for some serious high-level fishing. You can go cage fishing here for lobsters, and harpoon for tuna and swordfish. But this exotic island is about a lot more than fish. Take a walk through the jungle and check out the snakes and monkeys. You can find a lot of imps here, too. Maybe they like the frenetic energy on the island – random events seem to happen a lot on the fishing dock! If you want to escape the island for calmer ground, make sure you have another 30 GPs on you. The fare to get to the island covers only a one-way trip! It's worth noting that most of Karamja is accessible to members only, but there are many options that will make the trip worthwhile to free players as well.

Places to Shop
Karamja General Store

Places of Interest
Banana plantation, where you can pick free bananas
Fishing dock
Jungle
Volcano

People of Interest
Luthas, owner of the banana plantation. He'll give you a job if you need extra GPs.

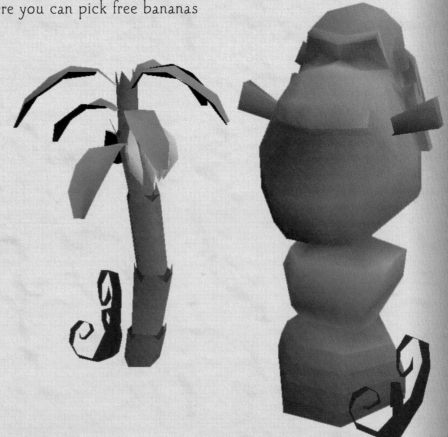

Crandor

Crafting
Guild

Melzar's
Maze

Rimmir

About Rimmington

This town is located west of Port Sarim. It's pretty much deserted, like a ghost town. Most people are just passing through on their way to the large mining pit north of the town. Even so, a few shops and businesses manage to survive.

Places to Shop

Brian's Archery Supplies
Rimmington General Store
Rommik's Crafty Supplies

Also Look For . . .

Cooking range
Onion and cabbage farms north of town
Water

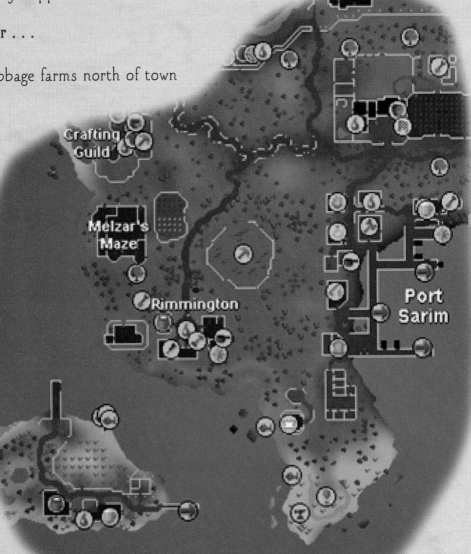

About Barbarian Village

This is the place to go if you want to battle with – you guessed it – Barbarians! Many players go here to practice combat, so you'll find a lot of Barbarian bones littering the ground. If you're not into battling, this is also a good place to come to practice crafts such as pottery and spinning. Otherwise, it's an uncivilized village, with only one place to shop. To find Barbarian Village, look between Falador and Varrock, along the river.

Places to Shop

Helmet Shop, so you can protect your head from Barbarian attacks

Also look for:

Fishing
Mining
Pottery oven
Pottery wheel
Spinning wheel

About Dwarven Mine

Head north of Falador to find a few buildings on top of a large and cavernous mine. You have to climb down through a trapdoor to get through the mine, but it's worth it. There, you can do your own mining, or buy ores in the underground shop. And you'll get to hang around a lot of dwarves!

Places to Shop
Ore Shop

Places of Interest
Next to the Dwarven Mine is a large monastery. The monks there will heal you if you are injured.

People of Interest
Nurmof, who repairs pickaxes in the Dwarven Mines

About Goblin Village

There's not much going on in this tiny village unless you're a Goblin. There are no shops but a few conveniences.

Places of Interest

In the center of the village is a fire that never goes out, which is handy if you need to cook something quickly.

People of Interest

You'll find Goblin generals Bentnoze and Wartface in the main building. You'll need to find them if you go on the Goblin Diplomacy quest.

About Edgeville

You'll find this small and quiet village north of Barbarian Village. It's close to the Wilderness, so you'll see a lot of fighters hanging out there, getting ready to battle.

Places to Shop

General Store

Places of Interest

Edgeville Dungeon, where you can fight monsters and mine
Edgeville Prison

People of Interest

Oziach, an armor maker you will meet in the Dragon Slayer's quest

Also Look For . . .

Bank, Barn, Range, Water, Yew trees

Random Events

Who doesn't like surprises? That's what random events are all about – strange events, characters, or creatures that come out of nowhere. Sometimes a random event can lead to a reward, and sometimes it can lead to trouble! Oh, well. Life would be boring if there were no surprises at all, right? Here's a look at the kinds of random events you can expect in the game.

Guardians

As you travel around the RuneScape world, you will come across some places that are protected. These Guardians are usually pretty powerful, and your best bet is to run away from them. They won't chase you for very long. Of course, you can always battle them if you are up to the challenge. They might drop some interesting items for you to collect. . . .

Golem

These rocky giants are powerful but slow and not too smart. You may disturb one while mining.

River Troll

Don't mess with a River Troll's fish! It will chase you away, although it won't move very far from the river.

Shade

A type of spirit that guards burial sites. You don't want to mess with these spooky creatures.

Tree Spirit

Watch out! That tree you just chopped down might be home to a Tree Spirit. And it's not too happy about losing its home. . . .

Zombie

Burying bones may strengthen your prayers, but you might attract one of these ghastly ghouls while you're at it!

Gift Givers and Helpers

These characters will either give you something good, or help you get out of a tight spot.

Certers

Following their retirement from the "certing" business, Niles, Miles & Giles have been seen wandering around RuneScape chatting to passing players. Talk to them and they might reward you, but if you fail their test, they'll try to convert items from your inventory into banknotes!

Drill Demon

The Demon Army wants you! Obey your sergeant, and you'll be rewarded with part of the Demon uniform.

Drunken Dwarf

If one wanders up to you, chat with him. He'll share his kebabs with you. Yum!

Evil Bob's Slaves

A strange cat will drag you off to a weird dimension to serve as his slave. You can escape if you get help from his other slaves.

Freaky Forester

This strange man may teleport you to a clearing in some distant forest to help him kill a pheasant. If you bring him the carcass of the correct pheasant, he may reward you with some of his uniquely rustic clothes.

Frog

You know the fairy tale–the one about the prince or princess being turned into a frog by an evil magician. The cure is usually a simple kiss. So if a small army of frogs comes to you, be prepared to smooch their leader!

Highwayman

Rick Turpentine spent years robbing the innocent. Now the notorious Highwayman wants to make up for his crimes. If he offers you some free valuables, take them! If you ignore him, he'll get angry and attack you.

Lost Pirate

When Cap'n Hand wants your attention, you'd better give it to him. He's an impatient fellow, and pirates are usually armed and dangerous.

Maze

If you get teleported into a Maze by some Mysterious Old Man, don't worry. You can escape the Maze when you find the center – and get a nice reward to boot.

Mime

If you get teleported to a mysterious theater, don't panic! All you have to do is follow the Mime's performance and you'll be released – along with a reward.

Mysterious Old Man

Don't be spooked by this guy – if you talk to him, he'll reward you with a Strange Box. If you ignore him, he'll teleport you into a Maze. There's a reward either way, but it's easier to solve the riddle of the Strange Box than to get out of the Maze.

Prison Pete

Get ready for another cat with bad intentions! This one drags you off to the mirror world of ScapeRune and locks you in jail. There you'll meet Prison Pete, who will help you find your way out. The keys to the prison portals are hidden inside little balloon animals scampering around the floor. Pull the big lever to see what sort of animal to pop.

Quiz Master

Odd One Out is the greatest quiz show in RuneScape. If you're lucky, the Quiz Master will invite you to compete for valuable prizes. If you get the questions right, you get a reward. But should you choose the cash prize or the mystery box?

Sandwich Lady

The Sandwich Lady loves to give out free snacks. Pay attention when she talks to you. If you take the wrong item from her tray, she'll get angry and may teleport you somewhere far away.

Strange Box

If the Mysterious Old Man gives you a Strange Box, get ready for a challenge! If you answer the question correctly, you'll get a reward. Be careful, though. A Strange Box will keep duplicating until your inventory is full!

Danger!

If you are unlucky enough to run into any of these events, run in the other direction!

Ent

Not all trees will let you chop them down. Some like to fight back!

Evil Chicken

What's so scary about a Chicken, you ask? Oh, if only you knew! This fiendish fowl can put up a tough fight.

Exploding Rock

Sometimes there are dangerous gases in mining sites. If a spark from your pickaxe ignites the gas, your pickaxe will get damaged. Fortunately Nurmof can repair pickaxes in the Dwarven Mines – for a price, of course.

Swarm

Swarms of insects can be dangerous. If you see one, run away until they leave you alone.

Whirlpool

When you're fishing, a sudden Whirlpool can suck your fishing equipment right out of your hands.

Just Plain Annoying

Just like in real life, sometimes things just go wrong.

Fishing

There are some big fish swimming around which don't like being caught. They might steal your equipment and spit it out nearby.

Lost & Found Office

RuneScape's public transportation system isn't perfect. If you're riding the Teleportation Matrix and find yourself stuck in some hole, don't panic. Just look at the nearby levers. Pull the one that is different to continue your journey.

Mining

If you swing your pickaxe too wildly, the head might fly off. Just pick it up, reattach it, and start swinging it again – but more carefully, this time!

Woodcutting

A faulty axe also can lose its head if you don't control your swing. If you pick it up and reattach it, you're back in business.

Glossary

As you travel around RuneScape, you will chat a lot with other players. Sometimes you won't know what they're talking about! You might also see terms in other places that you don't know. Here's a list of common RuneScape slang and terminology:

2H: Two-handed sword

Addy/Adam: Adamantite, a metal that many weapons and armor are made from

Ammy: An amulet,

Baxe: Battle-axe

Chain: Chainmail body

Choob: A high-level player who acts like a noob, or new player

Edge: Edgeville, a town in RuneScape

ESS: Rune essence

F2P: Free to play (non-members)

Fally: Falador, a city in RuneScape

Forge: To form metal into a shape by hammering it

GP: Gold piece

HP: Hitpoint

Jmod: Jagex staff member

Lobby/Lob: Lobster

Long: Long sword or longbow

Lumby, Lummy: Lumbridge, a town in RuneScape

Lvl: Level

Med: A medium helmet

Nats: Nature runes

NFS: Not for sale

Noob/Newbie: A new player

NPC: Non-player character

PK: Player killing

Pl8: Short for platemail body, a type of armor

P2P: Pay to play (members)

Pmod: Player moderator

Pots: Potions

Pure: Someone who specializes in a certain skill such as Magic or Woodcutting

QP: Quest points

RC: Runecrafting

RS: RuneScape

Scimitar: A long, curved sword. Also called scim, scimmy, skim, or skimmy for short.

Smelt: To melt an ore so you can separate the metal from it

Swordy: Swordfish

Tally: Talisman

WC: Woodcutting

Wildy/Wild: The Wilderness

X-bow: Crossbow

XP: Experience point(s)